MW01127289

Soulful Prayers for Women: Trusting God with Matters of Your Heart

Michele Teague-Humphrey

ISBN: 1544680678

ISBN 13: 9781544680675

What people are saying...

Circumstances change, situations surface, and uninvited issues inconveniently interfere in our affairs without notice. We make mistakes. Navigating our way through these vicissitudes and moving past our mistakes is challenging. In *Soulful Prayers for Women: Trusting God with Matters of Your Heart*, Pastor Michele Humphrey offers refreshing practical wisdom, powerful prayers, and impactful Scriptures to help women confront and conquer the disconcerting challenges we continually face. If you are seeking to be a victorious over-comer in all areas of your life, then *Soulful Prayers for Women: Trusting God with Matters of Your Heart* is a must read. The soul-stirring words and heartfelt prayers in this inspirational book will not only help you to heal, but encourage you to hang in there as you journey towards the unique destiny God has in store for you.

Dr. Alice Ridgill, Founding Pastor
New Faith Presbyterian Church
Greenwood, South Carolina

Soulful Prayers for Women: Trusting God with Matters of Your Heart provides a great platform for someone who is not sure how to take life's difficult issues to God. It gives the reader permission, and a foundation for learning how to share her most intimate problems with God. *Soulful Prayers for Women: Trusting God with Matters of Your Heart* reaches the reader physically, emotionally, and spiritually. As a professional counselor, I feel comfortable with endorsing this book with my clients and many others, trusting that it will lead them on a healthy pathway to healing, that is free from judgment or shame.

Martina S. Moore, PhD
President and CEO
Moore Counseling & Mediation Services, Inc.

God is our creator and the Great Heart Fixer. He has the answer to all of our needs. Pastor Michele Humphrey has taken the wisdom gained as a Shepherdess to guard our souls and direct us back to the Master. By shaping prayers, she carefully and gently herds us to focus with words of wisdom to reconnect back to our Power source. I am encouraged and excited to have these inspirationally designed "God-Rails" to remind me to run to the Savior.

Dr. Jacquelyne E. Bailey, Associate Pastor
The Lion of Judah
Inner-Healing Ministry
Cleveland, Ohio

In Memory of

Sherlean Hurry, my Mother
1949–2009

My greatest supporter, who believed that I could do anything!
I know that you are smiling down from heaven. I am smiling back.

Dedication

To my husband, Sylvester Humphrey, who would not let me forget that I had a book to write.

To my daughters, Ashley and Alayna. You had to endure my rambling about this book for years, and you never complained.

To Min. Angela Williams. You often saw things in me that I didn't see in myself. Thank you for the constant pushing, nudging, and reminder of the platform that God has called me to.

To Rev. Dr. Wanda Coleman. It's done after several years of broken deadlines!

To my girlfriends Rev. Courtney Clayton-Jenkins, Rev. Dr. Sabrina Ellis, and Rev. Renae Moore. You have inspired me and sharpened me to do better.

To Rev. Dr. Monte Norwood. Thank you for being my pastor and mentor! You invested in me and planted seeds in my soul that continue to grow and blossom.

To Lisa Hodges. You wore me down at times as you constantly chastised me for not completing the book.

To Michelle Eppinger, the sister I never had. Love you for life! You never allowed me to make excuses. Thank you!

Table of Contents

Foreword

There is no single recipe that has been given to us for prayer for every area of our lives. We are challenged each and every day with problems, issues, and concerns. The Bible teaches us to take our cares to the Lord. The world has taught us that sharing our hurt at times can be a painful event. We can experience rejection, shame, and even condemnation when sharing our pain with others. Having a place to take your concerns and lay them there completely and feel accepted is the way that God deals with our honesty.

The scripture that resonates for me when reading this book is 1 John 5:14 (NIV): "This is the confidence we have in approaching God: that if we ask anything according to his will, he hears us." This book is an introduction on how to come before God in the most sincere and transparent way, without being overly religious but truly sincerely seeking answers and affirmation from God. This book lets the readers know that they are not alone with real-life problems that many are afraid to discuss. It gives the readers permission to express themselves as never before and receive validation, love, forgiveness, hope, and healing. It is a great preparation for someone who needs emotional healing by starting with God and for someone leading them to professional help that will assist in completing the process. What an amazing truth to realize that our problems can be brought to God with openness. That we can be accepted by God even when we feel rejected by man. That our prayer life can lead us to healing, and a wonderful and full relationship with God.

Martina S. Moore, PhD
President and CEO
Moore Counseling & Mediation Services, Inc.

Introduction

Serving as an associate pastor and graduating from seminary prior to becoming a senior pastor of a church still did not adequately prepare me for what I would encounter serving as a pastor of a congregation. Of course I was aware of the numerous hours that would be required weekly to prepare a sermon and Bible-study lesson. I was prepared for the countless meetings, funerals, weddings, hospital visits, and baby blessings, as well as the countless other responsibilities and tasks that came with the position.

However, what I had not been adequately prepared for was the depth of people's pain, the masks that people chose to uncover before my eyes, and the demons that they battled with. The shock was not in their stories but the fact that they were willing to share things with me that I myself may have never had the courage to share with my own pastor or even a counselor for that matter.

It was in these meetings with various members of the congregation when I began to recognize that people were coming to church but not necessarily being healed. It was easy for them to come in wearing masks because many of the things that plagued their lives were rarely addressed. Stories that they shared in the confinement of my office were taboo subjects or topics that simply were not preached about. Sure I would preach occasionally on marriage, but never have I preached on what to do when you no longer love your spouse or how to get out of an affair when you really don't want to. Sure I preached on topics pertaining to singles but never on what to do when you are pregnant and you're not sure who the father is. Those who came into my office were battling issues that weren't even being battled in God's throne room. Because the church was silent on many issues, the people remained silent about their pain and their struggles, and they refused to even discuss them with God.

This posed a problem for me because we can never reach a level of intimacy with God if we are not willing to bear our souls to God. I am grateful for having a church where many are comfortable sharing their deepest and oftentimes darkest secrets with me, but I cannot be one's only stop for healing, deliverance, or breakthrough. I can provide spiritual guidance and pray for the emotionally and spiritually afflicted, but true deliverance takes place when you become a participant in your deliverance or healing. Even if my office is the first stop in which one confesses that they need help, God's throne room is where the miracle of deliverance and healing will take place. No matter how many people pray for you, until you begin to cry out to God for yourself, then and only then will you encounter the holy and divine God who is able to touch your soul like no one else can.

This book is to help you in your spiritual journey to complete wholeness in God. If there is no true authentic prayer life, there is no true relationship with God. Your relationship with God is going to make all the difference in the world, but it requires transparency. You must be honest with yourself and honest with God. You must share your heart, your pain, your fears, your struggles, and even your disappointments with God. Until we are comfortable going to God, crying out from the depths of our soul, and experiencing God's love, grace, and healing power, we will continue to live deficient lives as the people of God.

You may not have a church home or a pastor that you are comfortable in confiding with, but you have a God who desires to meet you where you are and to help you become more than you ever thought possible. You have a God who is listening.

How to Benefit from These Prayers

1. Not every prayer in this book will speak to your particular situation. Those particular prayers that do speak to your struggle or need may or may not address your need exactly. These prayers can be modified. Add your own words that reflect your particular situation. For instance, maybe the pain that you have endured is

not from an alcoholic mother but instead an alcoholic father. Use the same prayer, but substitute father and make the prayer applicable to your situation.

2. Allow this book to serve as a foundation for you to begin to write your own prayers, particularly if you feel at a loss for words when you attempt to pray. Writing down your prayers will help you to become more comfortable in expressing yourself. Once you have written a prayer, read it aloud to God. As you become more comfortable expressing yourself to God, you will no longer need to write down your prayers.

3. You will notice that these prayers are written in simple language. There is nothing eloquent about them. There are no big, fancy words. God wants to hear from your heart, and he wants you to express yourself in your regular everyday words. God is not impressed by our eloquence. God is blessed by our transparency.

4. Don't pray only once for a particular situation. Continue to pray for your situation until you feel a release from the prayer. When you have a sense of peace about what you have prayed for or you are able to see God at work in your life or situation, begin to thank God for what he is doing in your life.

5. As you skim the table of contents, you will notice prayers that cover a variety of topics. Let this book be a reminder to you that God wants to be involved in every area of your life. God wants you to call on him and to depend on him for help and guidance. Whatever bothers you, concerns you, or disturbs you, pray about it, and watch your relationship with God evolve to a new level.

6. Most of these prayers acknowledge God's love, power, or faithfulness, as well as our dependence upon God to meet our need. The prayer ends with our confession of trust, and it closes with praying in Jesus's name. When you begin to pray on your own, do not limit your prayers to problems and situations, but also give prayers of thanksgiving, acknowledging the wonderful things that God has done and is doing in your life.

7. These prayers do not necessarily replace the need for spiritual guidance from a pastor or the need to seek counseling from a licensed professional. Sometimes our pain is deep-rooted, and we need both prayer and wise counsel on our road to healing and deliverance.

~ Chapter One ~

Prayers for Your Children

Children are a heritage from the Lord,
offspring a reward from him.

—Psalm 127:3

Don't worry that children never listen to you;
worry that they are always watching you.

—Robert Fulghum

1. God's Blessing on Child's Life

Dear Lord,

Blessed be your name. For you are God, and we are your children created in your image and likeness. Thank you for making yourself known to me and for keeping me safe and secure all the days of my life. Thank you for being a kind and merciful God and for blessing me in so many ways, even when I was undeserving. As your daughter, I thank you for my children that you have blessed me with, but I also ask you Lord to bless my children. Bless my children to be respectful to their peers, to adults, and those in authority. Bless them, my God, to know you and fear you all the days of their life.

Be with my children, O Lord, and may others see that you are with them. May they excel in all that they do that brings glory to your name. May they be loving and kind to both friend and stranger. May they be generous with the material blessings that you graciously provide. May your hand be on my children to be leaders in the world yet followers of Christ.

May they have a heart to do right and never do anything out of selfish ambition or gain. May they be go-getters in life, hard workers, and servants in your kingdom.

May they feel your love, may they know your voice, and may they do well all the days of their life. In Jesus's name, Amen!

Scripture for Meditation

> "Then people brought little children to Jesus for him to place his hands on them and pray for them…"
>
> (Matthew 19:13).

Word of Wisdom

The best thing that you can do for your children is to be a praying parent and a positive role model! Be a godly example before them of how to treat others, how to handle conflict and problems, and how to share and give to others. Understand that children will sometimes make mistakes in life. Use their mistakes as teaching moments. Become your children's greatest supporter, but know when to extend tough love so that your children grow up understanding that with good or bad behavior comes good or bad consequences, respectively. Lastly, if you want your children to know God, be sure to take them to church or at least to teach them about God at home. You can do this by reading Scripture with them or by purchasing a children's Bible that is appropriate for their particular ages. Lastly, pray with your children. Incorporate prayer as part of your family's routine right before you put your children to bed or send them off to school.

2. Divine Protection

Dear God,

I thank you for the children that you have so kindly blessed me with. Thank you for trusting me to care for them, to nurture them, and the opportunity to raise them to become good, decent, and loving people. As their mother I will do my best to protect them, but, Lord, I need your help. I need you to watch over them day and night because I cannot always be with them every second or moment of the day.

I ask that you protect their minds and hearts from calloused words spoken by others that can injure their souls or self-esteem. I ask you, dear Lord, to protect them from family members and those who I trust, who may not have their best interests at heart. Please keep my children safe from monsters such as pedophiles, kidnappers, bullies, and anyone who seeks to abuse them.

I ask you, O Lord, that you protect them even from stray bullets, acts of violence, accidents, mishaps, and from crippling diseases and ailments that can rob them of a full and joyous life. Lord, hear my plea and keep my children safe each and every day. Thank you, my God, for hearing my prayer! In Jesus's name I pray! Amen!

Scripture for Meditation

"The Lord will keep you from all harm—he will watch over your life; the Lord will watch over your coming and going both now and forever more"

(Psalm 121: 7–8).

Word of Wisdom

Wouldn't it be wonderful to be able to watch and guard your children twenty-four hours a day? Wouldn't it be awesome to be able to foresee danger and hence protect your child? But unfortunately we don't have the capacity to protect our children twenty-four hours a day. However, you can train your child to be observant of their surroundings and to trust their instincts when something isn't right. Teach younger kids to not talk to strangers, and remind your teen the importance of not sharing personal information on social media and to not connect with strangers who may be disguised as someone who just wants to be a friend.

After you've taught and trained your children and you've prayed for them, put them in God's hands. Try not to spend all your time worrying about your children or becoming overly protective to the point that it interferes with your children or teens enjoying their childhood. We do not know what the future holds for our children, but we must take advantage of the moments that we are blessed to have them. Spend that time loving them, training them, and teaching them how to trust God and to live at their best potential. Don't worry about those things that are unfortunately beyond our control. Trust God.

3. Help with a Rebellious Child

Dear Lord,

You are my rock and shield. I call on you because you are my God. You fill my life with good things, and I give you praise. You lead me and guide me always in the right direction. You watch over my household day and night, and for that I am eternally grateful and thankful.

But, dear God, I am weary because my son/daughter is causing me and others problems because of his/her rebellious attitude. He/She is disrespectful and won't follow directions or the rules of the house. Lord, I need you to take a hold of (child's name), and steer him/her in the right direction. I am fearful that if he/she continues on this path that he/she may do something that he/she may later regret.

Please help me to show tough love and not to lower the standard or accept the behavior. Although I feel like I've done everything that I know to do, I ask for wisdom, but I also give him/her to you. I trust you, Lord, to do what I have no power to do. Save my child and get him/her on the right path! I thank you in advance for my child's deliverance. In Jesus's name I pray, Amen!

Scripture for Meditation

"Discipline your children, and they will give you peace; they will bring you the delights you desire"

(Proverbs 29:17).

Word of Wisdom

If you have a very rebellious child or teenager, check with your child's school, your county, or law enforcement to see if they have any special programs for rebellious or at-risk kids.

Also be sure to extend discipline when needed. Remember that discipline does not need to be physical. You can discipline your child/teen by taking away things such as toys, special privileges, cell phones, or special activities until their behavior improves and add things back gradually as a change of behavior becomes evident.

You may also want to talk with a school counselor to see if he or she may suggest that your child or teen be evaluated for an emotional, behavioral, or psychological disorder. Lastly, be sure to get the emotional and spiritual support that you may need too as you deal with the challenges of a rebellious child. It may be a good idea to see if you can find a support group for parents. Prayerfully this is just a phase that he or she will grow out of. Stay encouraged.

4. Better Relationship with Stepchildren

Dear God,

I thank you for the opportunity to come to you in prayer. I am humbled that you love me that much to want to commune with me and have conversation. I am also thankful that I can come to you, my God, about anything and everything.

That's why I come to you now, Lord, because I honestly need your help. Help me, dear God, to love my stepchildren. I thought that it would be an easy thing to do because I love their dad so much, but I have difficulty embracing them. I know that they are only kids and probably desire for their parents to be back together, which is why they don't seem to be receptive of me.

I notice that my mood changes when they are around because I feel like a third wheel. I know this is the wrong attitude to have, but our home seems much more pleasant when they are not around. Deal with me, Lord! Get my heart, my attitude, and my spirit right. Forgive me for feeling the way that I do. May I not act according to my feelings, but may I love them with your love and show kindness always. Most importantly, I pray to one day develop a wonderful relationship with my stepchildren. Thank you for hearing my prayer and getting me together! You are awesome, Lord. In Jesus's name I pray.

Scripture for Meditation

"Love must be sincere..."

(Romans 12:9).

Word of Wisdom

Blended families do not always blend well, whether it's stepchildren moving into the home or even just visiting on weekends. It takes time and patience for two families to blend together. You must remember that you and your spouse chose each other, but your stepchildren did not choose you. They may not love you because they do not yet know you. Realize that kids are experiencing all sorts of emotions, and most desire for their parents to be together.

Yes, it can be frustrating dealing with the attitudes, eye rolling, and disrespect from the stepchildren, but you and your spouse must work together in helping the kids to feel secure. Your children or your spouse's children should never feel as if they are losing a parent. They want to know that you can love them too and won't seek to take their dad away from them. Keep praying, love sincerely even through the emotions, and watch God move in your home. Do not underestimate the power of love.

5. Mourning Loss of a Child

My God,

I am overwhelmed with grief, sorrow, pain, and even anger. I can't understand why my child had to die. Why would you allow me the blessing of birthing a child just to one day take him/her away from me? I am so confused, and I just don't understand why this had to happen to me.

This pain is more than I can bear. I don't know if I can go on like this. How long will it hurt so bad? How long will I be tormented from the pain? Lord, you have to help me through this because if you don't, I will break. If you don't help bring me out of this darkness, I may never recover. If you don't heal my heart, I won't be able to get through this.

Help me, Lord! Give me the strength and desire to go on. Help me, God, to stand because I am so weak. Help me not to be angry with you, O God. Heal my soul. Help me, dear Lord! May I still trust you. May I still love you. Help me, Jesus.

Scripture for Meditation

"Precious in the sight of the LORD is the death of his saints"

(Psalm 116:15).

"Trust in the Lord with all your heart and lean not to your own understanding"

(Proverbs 3:5).

Word of Wisdom

I am glad that you took the time to pray despite your pain. Sometimes we are filled with so much grief, sorrow, or anger that we don't even want to talk to God. But even in the midst of your pain, it is important that you cry out to God because God will ultimately be your strength during this difficult time. God will lead you through the darkness and sustain you through the pain day by day.

Please consider grief counseling as you experience a wide range of emotions in the death of your child. Healing will not come quickly. It can be a rather slow process, and for many, the pain never goes away. They simply learn how to live with the pain in such a way that they are not left paralyzed by the pain but are able to continue with living.

Just know that God is with you, but also be open to the love and support of others. Even if others cannot understand your pain, their presence can be therapeutic, and their ear can be an opportunity to share memories of your child. Remember that you are never alone. God is with you, so don't be afraid to cry out to God, and somehow over time, God will empower you to move forward.

6. Patience in Parenting

Dear Heavenly Father,

Bless your name, for you are God, creator of heaven and earth. You are the sustainer of life and the God who holds all things together. And I call on you, God, because I need you to keep me together. I feel like I am losing myself. I love my children, but I am feeling overwhelmed, stressed, and burnt out. I just feel like I need room to breathe. It is as if my whole life revolves around them.

I have noticed that I have grown impatient with them. I've been yelling and screaming a lot because of my frustration, but I know that they are just being kids. So I am not asking in prayer for them, but I am asking you to strengthen me!

Dear God, give me the patience that I need. Help me not to lose my joy in parenting. Help me to cherish these moments that we have together knowing that one day they will be adults with their own families. Thank you, Lord, for not judging me but for giving me what I need. I love you, Lord. In Jesus's name I pray.

Scripture for Meditation

"The LORD is my strength and my shield; my heart trusts in him, and he helps me..."

(Psalm 28:7).

Word of Wisdom

Don't feel guilty when you become overwhelmed by the kids. It takes much time, energy, and patience to care for children. What I suggest to you is not only to pray (which you must continue to do for continued strength) but also make sure that you find some time for *you*! Invest in a baby sitter every other week for a few hours and go somewhere for "me time." If you are married, plan a date night with your spouse, and again, leave the kids at home with a sitter.

Just remember that being a parent does not mean that you must deprive yourself of some occasional fun or time away from the kids. In fact, why don't you call up a girlfriend and schedule a spa day or just a pedicure and lunch!

On another note, if you are feeling depressed or have thoughts of harming your kids, please seek counseling from a licensed counselor. Don't be afraid to seek help when you need it. That's the bravest thing that you can do.

7. Ability to Provide

Dear Lord,

Bless your name, for you are my God, and I worship you. I thank you for my life and that you allowed me to see another day. Thank you also for my children's life, for keeping them through the night, and bringing them home safely each day.

I call on you, Lord, because I am struggling to provide for my children. They need _____, and I don't have the means to provide. I don't want my children to suffer or to be without.

Your word tells me not to worry, but I am close to worrying, Lord. I don't know what to do or who to call. Please give me wisdom in this situation. Please provide for me and my children. I know that you are a God who desires that we call on you in our time of need, and so I give this situation to you. Thank you, Lord, that even now you are working it out for me. Thank you, my God, for hearing and answering my prayer! It is in my Savior's name that I pray! Amen.

Scripture for Meditation

"Do not be anxious about anything, but in everything, by prayer and petition, with thanksgiving, present your requests to God"

(Philippians 4:6).

Word of Wisdom

Pray for a blessing and expect a blessing because our God is a miracle worker, but in the meantime be proactive in doing what is necessary to find the needed resources and provision. Rather than sitting idle as you wait on God's blessing, check your county to see if there are any special programs that can assist you. If you need money, is it possible for you to hold a garage sale? Do you need to seek a second job temporarily to try and get on your feet until your blessing comes? While you are being proactive, expect to see God open doors or work through others to help provide with your needs. Remember, nothing is impossible for God!

8. My Teenager with Child

Gracious and merciful God, bless your holy name. Thank you for all that you are and all that you have been to me. Thank you for always loving me and never turning your back on me. You are worthy of all my praise.

I come before you as a parent crying out for my child. My child now has a child, and I am dealing with mixed emotions. For your divine purpose, you allowed this baby to be born and to be blessed with life, yet I see so many struggles ahead for my child as a young parent. I ask you, O God, to help my child be the best parent that he/she can be. Emotionally he/she was not ready for this, and, Lord, I was not ready for this either knowing that he/she would have to depend on me for guidance and support.

I pray that my grandchild will be loved, valued, and well taken care of by both his/her parents. I also pray that my child will continue his/her education and pursue his/her dreams although life may start off a little difficult.

Be with my child, dear Lord, and give him/her the maturity that he/she needs to raise my grandchild. Comfort and strengthen my son/daughter during any difficult times that he/she may face. Help me too, O Lord, as this affects my life as well. I love you and thank you for hearing my prayer. In Jesus's name I pray. Amen.

Scripture for Meditation

"He took a little child whom he placed among them. Taking the child in his arms, he said to them, 'Whoever welcomes one of these little children in my name welcomes me...'"

(Mark 9:36–37).

Word of Wisdom

Sometimes the plans that we have for our children don't work, but we must remember our own mistakes and shortcomings as well. Remember that many of us did not live our lives according to God's plans, yet God continues to love us. Therefore, be a supportive parent to your child.

Be careful not to become critical or judgmental of your child's mistake, and don't keep reminding him/her of his/her mistake. Refuse to complain about how this new baby affects your life. Trust me—your child is dealing with his/her own emotions in being a new parent as he/she now has the responsibility to care for a child.

As a parent be supportive, but of course set proper boundaries for your child so that your child is the one taking care of the baby. Love him/her the way that God loves you. Also, if your child is still sexually active, remind him/her of God's will for abstinence. However, if they choose to remain sexually active, greatly encourage him/her to use contraception. Lastly, don't forget to enjoy your new grandchild!

9. Healing of Ill Child

Eternal God,

You are the God of all creation, the originator of life, and the sustainer of life. It was you who created the world, created me, and created all that is. I call upon you, my God, because of your power to not only create but also to heal and restore.

My child needs your divine touch. My child is afflicted with a sickness that has taken control of his/her body, but I know that you are a God who can destroy sickness and disease. For you are all-powerful, and nothing can stand in your way!

My dear God, I ask you to heal my child's body and restore his/her health. Rebuke the sickness and disease that has taken up residence in my child's body. Protect my child from any other disease or sickness that seeks to invade my child's body!

Lord, destroy the disease from my child's body. Give my son/daughter complete healing and restoration so that his/her days on earth may be full and complete.

Thank you, my God, for responding to my prayer and for healing my child! In Jesus's name I pray!

Scripture for Meditation

"Praise the LORD, O my soul, and forget not all his benefits—who forgives all your sins and heals all your diseases"

(Psalm 103:1–3).

Word of Wisdom

Of course we know that there are times when God chooses not to heal; however, we walk by faith and not by sight as we hold on to the promises of God. Be sure to pray continuously for your child despite how things may look. God is indeed a healer, and you must trust that God will heal your child, whether through medicine, therapy, or supernaturally. Stand on God's word, pray with boldness, and believe in miracles!

10. Child with Behavioral Problem

My God in whom I trust, I give all honor, glory, and praise to you forever and ever! You have been my friend, my comforter, and my strength. I don't know where I would be without you.

Lord I come before you interceding for my child. I pray that you heal the source of his/her behavioral problems. I pray that (name of child)   will not always need medication or therapy to function normally. But if this is how you choose to heal him/her, then I pray that when he/she becomes an adult that he/she will continue the medication and therapy.

I also ask you, Lord, to give me the strength to care for and raise a child with behavioral problems, and help me to maintain peace in our home when my child's behavior is disruptive. Lord, please give the teachers the strength, patience, and compassion to work with my child. Protect my child from mockery and insensitivity from those who do not understand his/her condition. Also, give me the grace to care for my child.

May my child one day be able to function as a normal adult with or without the medication and to live a productive life. Thank you, as always, for hearing and answering my prayer. In Jesus's name, Amen.

Scripture for Meditation

> "Those who know your name trust in you, for you, Lord,
> have never forsaken those who seek you"

(Psalm 9:10).

Word of Wisdom

The fact that you have prayed this prayer tells me that you are not in denial about your child's behavior, but you also recognize your need for God's strength. It is not easy caring for a child or teen with behavioral issues of any sort, and I hope that you get the necessary support that you need in order to maintain your own sense of peace.

Do your best to be encouraging and supportive of your child, particularly if his/her condition is the result of disease, mental illness, a personality disorder, abnormal brain chemistry, trauma, injury, or anything that is beyond his/her control.

If your child's condition is due to rebellion, drugs, defiance, and such, seek professional advice on how to manage your child or to get him/her the necessary help that he/she may need. Although it may at times be tough, lean on God for continued strength and guidance. It's okay to lean on others too for continued support. As always, pray for God's divine healing, for we do not underestimate the power of God.

11. Child with Low Self-Esteem

Gracious and loving God,

Bless your holy name. You are God, and there is no one like you. You are the eternal, immortal, invisible, and wise God. I thank you that you are my God and that I am your child.

I come before you, dear God, to intercede for my child. My child has become so isolated from his/her peers and will not participate in many activities with others. Lord, (child's name) doesn't seem to have much enjoyment in his/her life.

I pray that my child can learn to love himself/herself and that he/she embraces his/her uniqueness. I pray, O God, that my son/daughter will not continue to measure himself/herself against others and to see himself/herself as insufficient, incomplete, or lacking because he/she doesn't measure up to a worldly standard.

Lord, please bring friends into my child's life who will love him/her for who he/she is. Please do not allow my child to be lonely. Lord, help my child to see just how valuable he/she is and how much he/she has to offer this world. Thank you, Lord, for your unfailing love for my child. In Jesus's name I pray. Amen.

Scripture for Meditation

"For you created my inmost being; you knit me together in my mother's womb. I praise you because I am fearfully and wonderfully made; your works are wonderful, I know that full well"

(Psalm 139:13–14).

Word of Wisdom

It can be difficult trying to encourage and motivate a child with low self-esteem. However, you may consider the following:

1. Is my child's source of low-esteem due to something that he/she can possibly change? For instance, lose weight if he/she is overweight. If so, as a family, work with your child on an exercise regimen along with healthy eating, and make it fun for the entire family.
2. Is my child's source of low self-esteem due to something that cannot be changed or easily changed? For instance, does your teen suffer from severe acne that is not responding well to treatment? Inform your child that chances are that they will grow out of it, and share your own insecurities you faced as a teen. If your child has a speech impediment or is extremely tall or short, teach them how to feel secure within themselves.
3. Does your child suffer from a social disorder? Seek professional counsel. Are they extremely shy? Maybe have a small sleepover at your house or some type of activity at the home, and invite a few other children to attend. This may help your child feel more secure since they are in a safe environment, and it may cause them to begin to slowly break out of their shell.
4. Continually affirm your child no matter their size, height, color, shape, or disability. Some things, your child may have to learn to

live with, but he/she also needs to understand that it is okay to be different, unique, or have certain limitations as long as it doesn't stop him/her from living a joyous and fulfilling life. Be sure to be supportive of your child and careful not to compare your child to any other children in the home. Lastly, do not forget the power of prayer.

12. Feeling Disconnected from My Child

Holy and magnificent God,

I come to you as my God, Abba, my Heavenly Father. For you are the keeper of my soul. You are my joy in life, and it is you, my God, who fills me with peace. I am grateful for your loving-kindness toward me and for always being there for me. I don't know where I would be without you, and I thank you that I am never alone.

I thank you, Lord, that I can talk to you about anything, even those things that are uncomfortable to talk about—uncomfortable because of the shame that I feel and sometimes the fear of being judged. But I trust that you are a loving and merciful God, who doesn't desire to judge me but to help me through my troubles and difficulties. So I come to you, O God, because I am feeling very disconnected from my child.

I don't know why I have difficulty embracing him/her. I feel like the bond that a mother and child are supposed to have is missing. I do love my child, but I find it difficult to tell my child that I love him/her. Lord, I don't want it to be this way. I don't want to be distant and disconnected from my child. I don't ever want him/her to grow up thinking that I don't love him/her. I guess I just don't know how to show it. Lord, help me to be a loving mother to my child the way that you are a loving Father to me. Help me to be able to show genuine affection and to be able to embrace my child. And lastly, Lord, I pray that one day my child and I will share an unbreakable bond.

I thank you, my God, for hearing my prayer, in Jesus's name. Amen.

Scripture for Meditation

"The eyes of the Lord are on the righteous, and his ears are attentive to their cry"

(Psalm 34:15).

"I call on you, my God, for you will answer me; turn your ear to me and hear my prayer"

(Psalm 17:6).

Word of Wisdom

It is difficult as a mother to admit to a broken bond or a bond that has never developed with your child, but you did it! Rather than pretending that everything is fine, you admitted to God that something is wrong in your relationship with your child. Despite feeling disconnected from your child, it is apparent that you do love your child and do want to have a better relationship with your child.

The question that you may have to ask yourself is, "Why am I feeling disconnected from my child?" Do you have an ill relationship with your child's father, and that affects your relationship with your child? Do you feel as if your child is a burden or has hindered your dreams or goals? Did you have a child sooner than you wanted to? Did you lack a close or loving relationship with your own mother?

Getting to the root cause of why you find it difficult to embrace your child may help you to understand what the hindrance or difficulty is. However, even if the reason is unknown, God is able to help us, heal us, and empower us in any area that we struggle in. I encourage you that if things don't seem to get better between you and your child, seek spiritual guidance from a pastor or counseling from a licensed professional. In the meantime, continue to pray, engage in fun activities to better connect with your child, and continue to rely on God's power.

13. For Forgiveness from Child

My Dear God,

I thank you for being my God. Thank you for loving me and forgiving me through your son, Jesus. I wish, dear God, that I can go back and erase the pain of the past, the pain that I have caused my child, but I know that I can't. However, I do ask, my dear God, that you touch my child's heart to forgive me.

I admit my mistakes and failures as a parent. I admit that I wasn't the mother that I should have been, and I know that I really hurt my child. But Lord, I pray that my child can realize how much I do love him/her. I pray that he/she will give me another chance and that we can have a true relationship.

Open my child's heart to allow me back in. Open his/her heart to give me one more chance. Open his/her heart to trust me again. And as you, O Lord, work on his/her heart and heal his/her pain, please continue to work on me to be a better mother. I thank you in advance for restoring our relationship. In Jesus's name. Amen.

Scripture for Meditation

"If we confess our sins, he is faithful and just and will forgive our sins and purify us from all righteousness"

(1 John 1:9).

Word of Wisdom

The hardest thing to do is not only to face your mistakes but to face the reality of the pain that you may have caused someone else, particularly your own child. It not only takes courage to confess your wrongs, but it also takes courage to stand back and allow the other person time to heal.

I encourage you to be patient with your child. Seek forgiveness, but also remember that your child must heal. Even if he/she forgives you, it may take time for your child to not only heal but to trust you again.

If your child does not seem receptive at this time to forgive you or to allow you back in, give him/her a little space, especially if this is an adult child. Don't be overly pushy or appear overly anxious for him/her to forgive you.

In the meantime continue to pray and allow your actions to speak for you so that your child can see that you have changed. Trust God to heal your child, and refuse to give up on healing and restoration of your relationship with your child. Lastly, forgive yourself so that you will not be overwhelmed with personal guilt and shame. Forgiving yourself is not to minimize the pain that you've caused but for the opportunity to find freedom and peace from the sins of the past.

14. Absent Father

My Father in Heaven,

Honor and glory to your name forever and ever. You are great and deserving of all honor and praise. I worship you as my God, and I surrender to your will. May I continue to draw closer to you and trust you in every area of my life.

Dear God, I come before you to pray for (child's father's name). I am frustrated and angry with him. He has not been faithful or committed to our child. He doesn't show up when he says that he will show up. He doesn't provide financial support. He keeps making promises and then breaks them.

Lord, what really hurts me is to see my child hurting. I pray, God, that (child's father's name) will wake up and realize that our child needs him and that he needs to become a better role model to our child. And, dear Lord, please help me not to become bitter towards him. Help me not to trash his name but to be respectful of him in front of our child. Lastly, Lord, I pray that despite how things may look now, my child will have a relationship with his/her father. I don't want my child to grow up bitter and angry that his father was not there for him/her.

Thank you, O God, for hearing my prayer. In Jesus's name. Amen.

Scripture for Meditation

"Hear me, LORD, my plea is just; listen to my cry. Hear my prayer—it does not rise from deceitful lips"

(Psalm 17:1).

Word of Wisdom

In situations like this, you must continue to pray and believe that your child will one day have a relationship with his/her father. What you don't want to do is to try and force a relationship. I know that you may not understand why your child's father would not want to be actively involved in his child's life, but for whatever reason, he chooses not to. You must accept this as your current reality, and rather than focus on the father's absence, focus instead on your opportunity to provide a loving and nurturing home for your child.

Also realize that having a child doesn't automatically make a person capable of being a father or mother. And despite your child's father not being in his/her life, pray that God will give you everything you need financially and emotionally as well as a support system of family and friends who can be there with you and for you as you raise your child.

Lastly, pray for God to heal your heart. You have a right to be angry with your child's father, but do not be ruled by that anger. Trust God in this situation, and continue to believe by faith that someday, whether sooner or later, your child's father will be active and devoted in his/her life. Even if your child's dad never lives up to his responsibilities, take pride in being the best mother, comforter, and provider that you could be for your child.

15. Drug-Addicted Child

Most holy and magnificent God,

I give you all praise as God of the universe and God of my life. I praise you because I have seen your works in my own life. I thank you that you have shown yourself to me on many occasions to let me know that you are real and that I am not alone. I thank you, Lord, that you are a God who cares about my life and that you are attuned to my emotions, my feelings, and my cries. I am crying out to you now, dear God, not for myself, but for __(child's name)__.

Lord, I need you to deliver __(child's name)__ from his/her addiction. I need you, my God, to set my child free from this bondage. Lord, remove the taste and the desire from him/her to do drugs. I ask, Lord, that you not only set __(child's name)__ free but also for him/her never to return to a life of drugs. Also, Lord, please remove my son/daughter from the wrong environment and friendships that help to feed into his/her addiction.

Lord, I know that you have a purpose for my child's life, and I ask you to open his/her eyes to see a great future ahead. Give __(child's name)__ a dream to pursue to help redirect his/her steps. I commit __(child's name)__ into your hands to heal and deliver him/her from this bondage of drug addiction. Thank you, O God, for hearing my prayer, and I trust that my prayer has already been answered. It's in Jesus's name that I pray.

Michele Teague-Humphrey

Scripture for Meditation

"The Spirit of the Sovereign Lord is on me…He has sent me to bind up the brokenhearted, to proclaim freedom for the captives and release from darkness for the prisoners"

(Isaiah 61:1–2).

Word of Wisdom

Whether your child is an adolescent or an adult child, it takes great patience, prayer, and emotional support as a parent to watch your child go through the many cycles of drug abuse or addiction. As a parent you will experience a range of emotions from guilt, as you wonder what you didn't do or could have done to prevent your child from taking a path towards drugs, to helplessness, as you witness your child hit a devastating low. Do know that, unless your child grew up in a drug-infested home, most likely you had nothing to do with your child's addiction. The reality is our children are oftentimes exposed to aberrant behavior outside of the home, and they sometimes become attracted to it.

If you truly desire to help your child, particularly if your child is a minor, you can consider a drug-rehabilitation facility. However, once your child is released, it will be up to him/her to put in the effort and boundaries that are needed in order to not fall back into addiction. Also know that addiction is a disease, and it needs to be treated as such. Medical treatment and possibly therapy with a counselor and spiritual support can help empower your child to overcome the addiction. Because I believe in the power of prayer, I encourage you to pray continuously for your child but also to get the emotional and spiritual support that you may need as a parent, since your child's addiction also affects you and the home.

16. Suicidal Child

My Father in Heaven,

I bless your name and honor you as my God. You are the one that I call on. You are the one that I depend on, and you are the one in which I place my trust. You, O God, are my rock and my strength, and I need you right now because I am overwhelmed with grief. Heavenly Father, I am emotionally distraught and feeling helpless for my son/daughter. I don't know what to do. I don't know where to turn or where to go. But mostly, Lord, I don't know how to help my child.

Dear Lord, I lift __(child's name)__ to you because he/she is depressed and feeling suicidal. I don't want to lose my child. I don't want to imagine __(child's name)__ leaving me, but I don't know how to help him/her. Lord, I am asking you to heal my son/daughter. Deliver __(child's name)__ from that dark place that he/she is in. Lord, if he/she is dealing with guilt that he/she doesn't know how to release, help him/her, O God, to find the forgiveness and peace that he/she needs. Lord if my child has been traumatized in some way that I am unaware of, please, Lord, reveal it to me. Whatever it is, Lord, my child needs you!

So, Lord, I ask that you block every attempt at suicide. I pray, God, that you set my son's/daughter's mind free of the thoughts of suicide. And lastly Lord, simply heal my child wherever he/she is hurting or feeling trapped. Thank you, my God. I don't know where I would be without you.

I bless your name forever and ever. In the name of Jesus the Christ, I offer this prayer to you.

Scripture for Meditation

"You, O Lord, keep my lamp burning; my God turns my darkness into light"

(Psalm 18:28).

"Then they cried to the Lord in their trouble, and he saved them from their distress. He brought them out of darkness and the deepest gloom and broke away their chains"

(Psalm 107:13–14).

Word of Wisdom

As a parent, the best thing that you can do is to be there for your child or teen. Let him/her know how much you love him/her, how important he/she is to your life, and how much of a blessing and gift he/she is to you. Be a listening ear to your child without critique, criticism, or judgment. Even if you cannot understand what they are feeling, acknowledge his/her feelings or pain and provide sympathy. Rather than trying to minimize his/her emotions, thank him/her for sharing and let him/her know that you are there with him/her and for him/her and that together the two of you can work through it. Also be sure to spend quality time with your child or teen that includes fun activities that you can do together as mother and child.

Lastly, be sure to talk to your child's or teen's physician for a medical examination or possible referral to see a psychologist or psychiatrist. Your child may be suffering from depression, which may require counseling and medication. Or you may discover that your child or teen has mental illness as the root cause of their suicidal thoughts. Sometimes love is not enough to prevent suicide. Therefore, combine prayer, spiritual support for yourself, emotional support, and a mental-health professional to help bring forth the healing and restoration that your child needs.

17. Incarcerated Child

My Beloved God,

Honor and praises belong to you, for no one is like you in all of heaven or on earth. You are a gracious, kind, and merciful God. You do not treat us as our sins deserve, and you have shown us the depth of your love by sending a Savior into the world to rescue us from sin and death. Thank you, dear God, for your mercies that are new every morning and for a perfect love that cannot decrease or increase. I thank you, my God, for loving us when we could not love ourselves.

And because of your unfailing love, dear God, I pray for your mercy toward my son/daughter. Lord, I make no excuse for my child, but I ask you, O God, to protect and keep him/her while behind bars. Protect __(child's name)__ from attacks from other inmates. Protect __(child's name)__ from being further corrupted or hardened while behind bars.

I ask you, O Lord, to reach __(child's name)__ while he/she is in prison. Speak to him/her so that it is evident that it is your voice he/she hears. Open my child's eyes so that he/she can see you clearly and the future that you have destined for him/her. But also, Lord, help __(child's name)__ to recognize the wrong that he/she has done and the pain that he/she has caused. Help my child to recognize that this is not the life that you have called him/her to. Save my child, Lord! Turn his/her life around, Lord! When __(child's name)__ is released from prison, let him/her come out as a new person in Christ!

Thank you, my dear God, for hearing the prayer of this concerned mother. I love you, my Lord. It is in the name of my Lord and Savior Jesus Christ that I pray.

Scripture for Meditation

"He will not always accuse, nor will he harbor his anger forever; he does not treat us as our sins deserve or repay us according to our iniquities"

(Psalm 103:9–10).

"...He has sent me to proclaim freedom for the prisoners..."

(Luke 4:18).

Word of Wisdom

No parent ever envisions his or her child one day being behind bars for a crime the child has committed. Yet our prisons and jails are filled with sons and daughters who decided to choose a path that leads to destruction. Some are on death row, some are incarcerated for life, some must do hard time, and others are there for a shorter period.

Regardless of where your son or daughter may fall, be sure to still be a mother to your child. When possible, try to make a visit to see your child to let him/her know that you have not forsaken him/her. A visitation does not mean that you condone his/her actions, but it does mean that you still love him/her even if you do not approve of the path that he/she has taken. God expects us to visit even those in prison (Matthew 25:34–46).

Also remember your son or daughter on his/her birthday by sending a card and letter in the mail. On your birthday or special occasions, send pictures from the family. Let your child know that even while behind bars, God loves him/her and that he/she is not forgotten or forsaken.

18. Prayer for Adult Child Facing Troubles

Gracious and loving God,

I come before you in reverence and humility, acknowledging your holiness and sovereignty. I worship you, for you are deserving of all honor. Who can compare to you? Who can love us the way that you do? Although we cannot fully fathom all that you are, I am grateful and thankful that you have given us a glimpse of yourself through your Son, Jesus Christ.

I come before you, my God, to lift up _(child's name)_ . Because you are a God who knows all things, you already know what he/she stands in need of. I am limited in my knowledge of all that _(child's name)_ is going through, but I do know that he/she needs you. I ask you, O God, that my son/daughter turns to you with his/her struggles and troubles. I pray that he/she comes to discover you as a God who cares about everything that he/she is going through, and that he/she doesn't have to carry his/her burdens alone.

I pray that _(child's name)_ will trust you with his/her problems and realize that you are his/her help in times of trouble. I ask you as a mother, dear Lord, to reveal yourself to my child as a provider and sustainer. Fill _(child's name)_ with wisdom and guide his/her steps according to your will. Help him/her to find peace in you during this difficult time, O Lord.

I thank you, Lord, for hearing my prayer, in Jesus's name.

Scripture for Meditation

"This poor man called, and the Lord heard him; he saved him out of all his troubles. The angel of the Lord encamps around those who fear him, and he delivers them"

(Psalm 34:6–7).

Word of Wisdom

Choose to be available to your adult son or daughter when your advice is warranted or needed, but do not become overbearing or feel that you must "fix" your child's life or problems. You don't want your adult child to be dependent on you, but instead he/she must be dependent on God. Help when it is in your power to help, but also recognize when it is time for your child to learn how to stand on his/her own two feet.

Rather than always seeking to rescue your child, offer to pray for your son or daughter and ask God to fill him/her with wisdom and knowledge. Also share your personal stories of times that you struggled and how God helped you to overcome. By your prayers and your own testimony, you want your child to see the importance of having faith in God.

If your child does not have a relationship with God and is not open to prayer, do not underestimate the power of a praying mother! In your private time, continue to lift your child's name to the Lord, and have faith that God will open your child's eyes and lead him/her on the right path. With God all things are possible.

19. My Child's Salvation

My Dear God,

I sing praises unto you. I lift your name on high, and I worship you as God of all creation and surrender to you as my Heavenly Father. You are my world, and you fill my life with peace and joy. You, O God, have saved me through your Son, Jesus, and you have given me purpose for living. Thank you for your unfailing love that manifests itself in innumerable ways in my life. You have been good to me and have shown me what true love is.

But, Lord, I want my child to have the same love that I have for you and the same hope that I have in you. I want my child's life to be filled with the peace and joy that I live with each day that comes from knowing you. I want my child to know that you are real and that there is life after this world.

I ask you, my dear God, to open __(child's name)__'s eyes to see you. Give my son/daughter spiritual sight to see beyond the realities of this world to something greater and permanent. Soften __(child's name)__'s heart to receive you. Please, dear God, do not let my son/daughter leave this world without receiving Jesus Christ as his/her Savior. Let him/her experience the undeniable power of your love that forever transforms our lives.

I place __(child's name)__ in your hands, O God, believing that one day my child will worship you as his/her God. I graciously thank you for hearing my prayer. It is in the name of the resurrected Christ that I pray. Amen.

Scripture for Meditation

"For I am not ashamed of the gospel, because it is the
power of God for the salvation of everyone who believes:
first to the Jew, then for the Gentile"

(Romans 1:16).

Word of Wisdom

Keep praying and believing for your child's salvation, and allow the presence of God to be seen in your daily walk as a witness to God's power and love in your life. Be sure not to badger your child, but instead pray for your child, love your child with the love of Christ, and be patient with your son/daughter just as God has shown you patience in your life.

20. To Be a Positive Example to My Child

My Heavenly Father,

You are the God of all. For there is nothing made that you have not made. You are creator and sustainer of life. It is you, my God, who watches over us and guides us in accordance to your purpose for our lives. I am grateful and thankful that you have opened my eyes and heart to see and know that you are real. Thank you, my God, for loving me and for showing me that there is no life without you.

Dear God, I come before you as a mother who is concerned about setting the right environment for my children. I want my home to be filled with your love and for my children to feel your love. I also want to be a mother who can be a positive example before her children. Lord, you know that I have made many mistakes in my life, and I am still not all who I need to be, but I pray for the sake of my children that I can be a positive role model and influence. Lord, I have already made some mistakes, but help me, O Lord, so I can guide my children not to repeat my mistakes.

I ask you, O God, to help me to be a mother my children can be proud of. I don't want my children growing up with mommy issues. I want my children to be able to talk about the love experienced growing up. I want my children to know that I sought to be the best mother that I could possibly be. Lord, I am not asking for perfection,

I am asking you, my God, to help me to not to be a stumbling block or hindrance to my children's emotional development or stability. Help me please, Lord, to be a mother who empowers, educates, and equips her children to become the very best that they can be in you. As you continue to work in me, my Lord, may my children reap the benefits.

Thank you, my Heavenly Father, for hearing my prayer. It is in the name of my Lord and Savior Jesus Christ that I pray. Amen.

Scripture for Meditation

"Let your light shine before others, that they may see your good deeds and praise your Father in heaven"

(Matthew 5:16).

Word of Wisdom

What a wonderful desire to have, to be the best mother that you can possibly be! But understand that even the best mothers sometimes make mistakes. Yet mistakes can be beneficial in your children's development when you use those mistakes to teach your children that everyone makes mistakes but that God forgives us and allows us the opportunity to do better the next time around. Try not to overthink motherhood, but learn as you go. Take motherhood one moment at a time. Rather than being weary of whether or not you are doing things right, simply seek to love your children and find joy in parenting. Your love will make all the difference in their world!

~ Chapter Two ~

Prayers for Your Marriage

*However, each one of you also must love
his wife as he loves himself, and the wife
must respect her husband.*

—Ephesians 5:33

*A successful marriage is an edifice
that must be rebuilt every day.*

—Andre Maurois

21. Unhappy in Marriage (Reason Unknown)

All-powerful and all-knowing God, I call on you because you are a great and mighty God. You are so loving and faithful. I am forever grateful that you are nothing like me. That is why I adore you and worship you. There is no love like yours.

My Father, I call on you because I need your strength, wisdom, and guidance for my marriage. I am not even sure if my marriage is the problem or if it is just me, but I am so unhappy, Lord. I just don't feel the way that I used to about my marriage or my husband.

It seems that my heart has changed so much. I thought that this was something that I wanted forever, but I am not sure if I want to continue in this marriage. It really isn't anything that he has done or hasn't done, but my heart has just changed.

I feel like I am faking happiness, and I know it is unfair to my husband. But I can't help feel what I feel, which isn't really anything. I feel nothing toward my husband or this marriage. Help me, Lord, in this matter because I don't want to stay in a relationship where I am not happy. Please speak to me, Lord. In Jesus's name I pray. Amen.

Scripture for Meditation

"Hear, O Lord, and be merciful to me; O Lord, be my help. You turned my wailing into dancing; you removed the sackcloth and clothed me with joy"

(Psalm 30:10–11).

Word of Wisdom

First of all let me suggest to you not to run or walk away from your marriage. Marriages go through seasons of excitement and boredom as well as adventure and monotonous routine. Marriages also have ups and downs. And despite all the highs and lows of marriage, we also have a wide range of emotions and feelings that we experience in the midst of married life.

Therefore feelings alone should never be the reason to give up on a marriage. If you are feeling unhappy, could it be that it has nothing to do with the marriage itself but everything to do with you? Have you possibly lost your identity? Have you stopped doing things that you once enjoyed doing? Are you pursuing your dreams even in the midst of being married? Has life become boring because you have fallen into a routine?

It is possible that when you are able to get in touch with your emotions and discover why you are unhappy—once you deal with the root cause—it may help to restore the joy in your marriage. Possibly consider going to see a counselor, who may help you to recognize the reason for the unhappiness. Remember, it takes a happy person to help create a happy marriage, but it also takes faith in God and patient endurance until a change comes. Continue to cry out to God, seek guidance, and try not to rush into any decision to leave your marriage.

22. Sexless Marriage

My Dear God,

Thank you for another day of life, and thank you, Lord, that you have given me everything that I need to have a successful day. However, I need your help to have a successful marriage. Lord, I don't know what happened to the love and passion that has resulted in our sexless marriage. I love my spouse, and I desire my spouse, but we have not made love in quite some time.

I don't know if there is something about me that turns him off. I don't know if I appear uninterested, or if he is having a problem sexually or is just not interested in sex anymore. Maybe we just need our love rekindled. I honestly don't know what the problem is, but I do know that those times that we have had sex, it was so lifeless.

Help us, O God. I really do love my spouse, and I have no desire to leave my marriage nor do I have a desire for anyone else. I pray, O God, that you help restore our passion and desire for one another. Help us, Lord, in this difficult time. I thank you that you are going to help turn my marriage around. In the mighty name of Jesus, I pray.

Scripture for Meditation

"The husband should fulfill his marital duty to his wife, and likewise the wife to her husband. The wife's body does not belong to her alone but also to her husband. In the same way, the husband's body does not belong to him alone but also to his wife"

(1 Corinthians 7:3–4).

Word of Wisdom

It may be time to have an honest conversation with your spouse and share your feelings and concerns. Hopefully your spouse will be honest and forthright. If not, pray for discernment, and ask God to give you clarity. It may also be possible that your husband's libido is not what it once was. He could be suffering from impotence or taking medications that may affect his sexual arousal or ability to perform. In those cases you must be sensitive to what he is going through but also encourage him to talk with his doctor. There are now medications on the market that can help with erectile dysfunction if that is the source of the problem.

If your husband is not willing to talk about the lack of passion and sex in the marriage or even refuses to admit to a problem, you can always suggest marriage counseling for both of you. Continue to pray that your husband will do what is necessary to restore the passion in the bedroom.

23. Husband's Salvation

Dear Heavenly Father,

Bless your holy name. Honor and praise belong to you, for you are the God of the universe, and it is you who gives life. I thank you for my life and that you opened my eyes and my heart to see you and know you. Thank you, God, for my salvation through your Son, Jesus. Thank you for giving my life purpose, significance, and meaning. I honestly don't know where I would be without you.

But, Lord, this prayer is not for me but for my husband. I am asking that you touch his heart. Help him to be able to see you and to hear your voice. Let him know just how real you are. Help ___(husband's name)___ to recognize his need for you. I know that you are real and that you are good, but I need him to know it too.

And help me, O God, not to badger him with his need to know you. As I step back, please do whatever you need to do to get his attention. Even if he won't listen to me, you know how to reach him. I ask you, Lord, please do not let my husband leave this earth without knowing you and calling your name. I thank you in advance for my husband's salvation. In Jesus's name. Amen

Scripture for Meditation

"For God so loved the world that he gave his one and only Son, that whoever believes in him shall not perish but have eternal life"

(John 3:16).

Word of Wisdom

The best thing that you can do for your husband is to pray for him and to allow God's light to shine through you. The last thing that you want to do is badger him about church or God because that can become the very thing that keeps your husband away. You also must be careful not to show disdain toward his behavior or make negative comments toward his attitude, even if it does not line up with God's will. Remember how you were before you came to know Christ?

You must show love, patience, kindness, grace, and mercy, just as Christ did for us when we were far from Him. We don't all come to Christ at the same time, and some may never come to Christ. We, however, have a responsibility as believers to model Christ before others, especially those who are unsaved. So rather than hounding your husband about knowing God, let your light shine so that he can see the benefits of having Christ in your life. The goodness of God should spill over into his life through you. So in the meantime be patient. Pray. Watch God move! Stand back and trust God!

24. My Secret Affair

O Merciful God,

I come before you, God, acknowledging that I am living outside of your will. I acknowledge my unfaithfulness to my spouse. I acknowledge that adultery is a sin against you and my spouse. I know that I should be able to just walk away from this affair that is against your will, but I can't and don't even know if I want to. I know what your will is. I know that it would hurt my husband if he found out. I know that this is wrong on every level.

Help me, dear God, to just walk away, to end it, and to be faithful to (husband's name). Help me to no longer desire this other person or at least to have the strength to not act on those desires. Deliver me from this sinful behavior and act of betrayal against my husband. Forgive me, O God, for what I have done to myself, to you, and to my marriage. Give me the strength to do what's right.

Forgive me, Lord.

Scripture for Meditation

"Marriage should be honored by all, and the marriage bed kept pure, for God will judge the adulterer…"

(Hebrews 13:4).

Word of Wisdom

Confession is the first step toward deliverance, but it cannot be the only step. You have taken the first step by acknowledging that adultery is wrong. It destroys the bond between a husband and wife and destroys families. Adultery puts you and your spouse at risk for sexually transmitted disease and at risk of the person who you are seeing to cause additional havoc on your marriage.

Now that you have made a confession to God about this relationship, it is up to you to do whatever is necessary to break away from it. God can forgive you when you walk away from it, but God cannot forgive you while you are still in it. You must then make the decision on whether or not to share this affair with your spouse. Not sharing this information can leave you with guilt and a secret that will eventually eat away at you. Also, the person you were having the affair with may decide to tell your spouse one day.

Even when God forgives us, sometimes we still face consequences of our actions. Know that revealing this information to your husband may lead to separation or worse, divorce. The truth is, nothing good can come out of adultery. Again, now that you have prayed to God, walk away from the affair, and then ask God to heal and restore your marriage after any fallout that may occur. Believe in God's healing and restorative power, but do understand that once the trust has been broken, even if your husband forgives you, it may take several years to rebuild. Also be sure to confront the issues that led you to an extramarital affair.

25. Abusive Relationship

Dear God,

I know that this isn't the life that you created me for. I know that you didn't give me life just for me to be hurt and abused by the one that is supposed to love me. You're a good God, so I know that this cannot be your will for my life, but I don't know how to get out. The truth is, I just wish ___(name)___ would get some help so that we can have a marriage that honors you.

What do I do, Lord? Where do I go? Who do I turn to? I don't want to go to a shelter. I don't want to even tell my family. I am afraid that if I stay, I may never get out, but if I leave, I may come back. Lord, help me to be strong and to love myself too much to settle for a life that causes me so much pain. Give me wisdom to get the help that I need for my own safety, and I pray that he gets help and deliverance as well.

Thank you, Lord, and I trust that you will save me but that I will also welcome your help when you send it.

Scripture for Meditation

"'For I know the plans I have for you,' declares the Lord, 'plans to prosper you and not to harm you, plans to give you hope and a future'"

(Jeremiah 29:11).

Word of Wisdom

You must ask yourself, "Is this the life that God has planned for me? Is it God's will that I suffer from abuse?" I believe that you already know the answer to these questions. No! God is a loving God, and although bad things happen in life, there are some things that we can escape by having the courage to walk away from, such as domestic violence.

I encourage you to seek help and then to accept the help that is offered. If you have children, another question that you must ask is, "Is this the kind of life that I want my children to witness, and do I want them to grow up believing that abuse or violence is acceptable?" Do what you must do to get to a safe place for you and your children if you have any. Remember, God is with you, and God will give you everything that you need should you decide to seek the life and future that God has destined for you. The number to the 24-7 National Domestic Violence Hotline is 1-800-799-SAFE (7233). You must make the decision yourself on whether or not to call.

Lastly, pray for your husband. Your husband is in a dark place, and he needs saving. Pray for his salvation and deliverance, but in the midst of praying for him, seek safety and refuge for yourself. While you are trusting God to work on him, trust God's provision as you seek safety.

26. Constant Arguing and Fighting

Most holy God,

You are my God, my comforter, and my peace. It is you who keeps me sane and keeps me holding on. It is you, O God, who strengthens me when I am weak and picks me up when I am down. I call to you, dear God, because I need you once again. We need you, Lord! Our marriage needs your healing touch, for all we do is argue and fight. We just can't seem to get along anymore.

Lord, please fix my marriage. Show us what we are doing wrong. Reveal to us what is broken, and then help us to heal and overcome. Somehow, Lord, we have lost our way. Somehow we have allowed the enemy to come in and cause division. But, Lord, you called us to be one. You called us to work together and to look out for each other. Help us, dear God.

If I am at fault in some sort of way then open my eyes so that I can see the part that I play. If my spouse is at fault then open his eyes too. I am praying to you, O God, because I do want my marriage to work, but I don't want to live like this. Help us to love each other the way that you love us. Help us to look beyond one another's faults and recognize each other's needs.

Thank you, Lord, as I trust you to help bring peace into our life. I love you, my God. In Jesus's name I pray! Amen.

Scripture for Meditation

"In your anger do not sin: Do not let the sun go down while you are still angry."

(Ephesians 4:26).

Word of Wisdom

The arguing may be a symptom of something that has gone wrong or is going wrong. The arguing may point to a place of tension or contention that has been overlooked, maybe because it is something that has been ignored over time. Until you get to the source of why the two of you are suddenly arguing or fighting, you both need to sit down and have honest dialogue and reflection.

Are there money problems or burdens that may have one of you on edge? Does it seem like someone is not pulling their weight in the household or marriage? Are there children in the house and time together is interrupted or seldom? Is someone experiencing stress at work, and the frustration is taken out on the other? Is there a need being neglected that seems to be ignored in the marriage? Regardless of any problems that there may be, it doesn't mean that you have to fight and yell at one another. Respect each other, and show kindness to one another. Represent Christ in how you treat each other. Problems cannot be an excuse to argue and scream at each other.

Lastly, talk out your problems. If you both cannot determine what the problem is, pray together for a certain period, asking God to heal your marriage.

27. Blessing for Marriage

Gracious and loving God,

How wonderful is your name! You are an amazing God, and I thank you for your unconditional love. And I pray, O God, that my marriage can have that kind of love, a love that is faithful, caring, patient, and forgiving.

I ask that you bless our marriage so that it is filled with joy and happiness. May it be a marriage that honors you in the way in which we love each other and treat one another. In a world filled with divorce and infidelity, protect our marriage, dear God, from the enemy, who seeks to destroy marriages.

Help us to set boundaries around our relationship. Help us, my God, to not allow outside influences into our home. May you be the One that we turn to when we find ourselves facing a storm or troubles. May we be faithful to each other and not forsake our vows that we made to one another on our wedding day.

Bless our marriage, our home, our family, our health, and our finances. I pray, dear God, that our marriage will not only be an example of a marriage rooted in Christ but a marriage that brings a smile to your face.

Love you, my God, in Jesus' name.

Scripture for Meditation

"May God be gracious to us and bless us and make his
face shine on us"

(Psalm 67:1).

Word of Wisdom

Today's marriages don't seem to last as long anymore. Divorce is oftentimes seen as a way out when you don't want to fight for your marriage or don't believe that the marriage can be saved. But a marriage
can work! However, it takes two individuals giving their all to make the
marriage what they desire for it to be. It means forgiving each other when
mistakes are made. It means being one another's greatest supporter or
cheerleader, and it also means being proactive in keeping others outside
of your relationship.

If you want God to bless your marriage, God will need cooperation
from both of you. You must value your marriage and tend to one another's
needs in the relationship. Your marriage can be all that you ever hope for
it to be as long as you both stay diligent in creating a loving relationship
and home. And lastly, when troubles come, don't allow troubles to divide
you, but rather, work together as one to resolve any problems. Keep God
in the center of your relationship by inviting God in through prayer.

28. Alcoholic Husband

Dear Lord,

I call on you as my God because you created me, and you know me. It is you who keeps watch over me and protects me. I acknowledge that it has been your hand guiding my life even when I didn't even really know you. Thank you for being there for me. You are truly a good God.

I come before you to pray for ___(spouse's name)___ because he is an alcoholic. I know it, and everyone else knows it, but he will not admit to it. I love my husband, but I don't like the drinking and all that comes with it. I don't like his change in attitude and behavior that can sometimes be vile and vulgar.

Lord, I need you to step in. I need you to intervene and save him before the alcohol kills him or destroys our marriage. I am truly trying to hold on as best as I can, but I am tired of the turmoil, chaos, and lack of peace in my home because of his drinking.

Please, God, get ___(spouse's name)___'s attention! Open his eyes to see the damage that he is doing to himself, our home, and our marriage. Deliver him, please God, from this addiction! I know that you hear my prayer and that you will step in and set my husband free.

As always, thank you, God, for being available to hear my prayers and cries. I love you. It is in Jesus's name that I pray. Amen.

Scripture for Meditation

"The Spirit of the Lord is on me...He has sent me to proclaim freedom for the prisoners and recovery of sight for
the blind, to set the oppressed free"

(Luke 4:18).

Word of Wisdom
Unfortunately, alcoholism is a progressive disease that will only get worse
if left untreated, and the problem is, your husband has to acknowledge
that he is an alcoholic and that he needs help. Even if your husband believes that he can stop drinking on his own, the truth is he is powerless to
do so. You may have already discovered this with his many broken promises to quit. There are Alcoholic Anonymous groups that have helped
millions to overcome drinking problems or have helped people to develop
coping skills to help overcome emotional triggers that could lead back to
drinking.

However, until your husband is willing to acknowledge that he is an alcoholic and needs help, the question that you must ask yourself is, "How
long do I suffer and put up with my husband's ill behavior?" Sometimes,
alcoholics neglect help because they don't see the effects of their behavior. As long as they still have a home, a wife, and a job, then they can feel
that they have a handle on their drinking. Oftentimes family and friends
enable the alcoholic to continue his or her drinking without consequences. Is it time for your spouse to face consequences to see that you are
serious about his need to get help? Pray continuously. Protect yourself
and children in the household, who may be affected by your husband's
drinking.

29. Healing from Infidelity

Dear Lord,

When will the pain ever end? When will my heart heal? When will I be able to trust again? I am so hurt, God, and I am really trying to forgive my husband, but I feel like I have been stabbed in my heart. How do I trust someone who has betrayed our marriage? How do I know that he won't do it again?

I am trying so hard, God, to forgive. I really am, but sometimes I want him to hurt just as badly as I hurt. Just the thought of him being with someone else drives me crazy. Please help me, Lord. Please help me to heal and my marriage to heal.

Help me not to blame myself for his need to go outside of our marriage. Help me, dear God, not to feel insecure wondering if I could have done something to keep him faithful. Lord, I need you to put a smile back on my face, put joy back into my heart, and peace back into my home.

I know, Lord, that I am not alone and that you will continue to comfort me, strengthen me, and get me back to a place of wholeness. Thank you, Lord, for being my rock, in Jesus's name.

Scripture for Meditation

"He heals the brokenhearted and binds up their wounds"

(Psalm 147:3).

Word of Wisdom

When you took your wedding vows, you never imagined that the vows you and your husband made to one another would one day be broken. Unfortunately, we never know what the future holds for us, and as imperfect people, we don't know beforehand the mistakes that we will make. Nor do we know the pain that we will experience oftentimes from those whom we love most.

Do know that you have the right to be angry and hurt. Adultery is painful because there is a violation of boundaries, and it destroys the trust in the relationship. I encourage you to grieve, but I also encourage you to seek emotional support from a trustworthy friend and possibly counseling, even if it is by yourself, to help you with the pain that you are experiencing.

Whether you choose to fight for your marriage or walk away from your marriage is up to you. However, should you choose to fight for it, it will take much energy, and it will be an emotional rollercoaster ride as you go through the process of healing. You may want to consider marital counseling for the two of you so that it can be determined how the marriage got to this point. Lastly, continue to pray to God. Lean on God for the spiritual support that you need and the healing that is possible through God, for there is no pain or marriage that God is unable to heal!

30. Husband with Cancer

Most holy God,

I praise your holy and precious name. I give you glory for all that you are and for all that you have done in my life. I recognize, God, that you have always been with me. You have always been someone whom I could turn to and someone whom I could lean on. You have been my strength through difficult times, and I need you, dear Lord, once again to help me through this difficult time.

I need you to heal my husband, dear God. I need you to touch __(spouse's name)__ 's body and heal him of the cancer. I know you have the power to heal him, my God. I know that your power is stronger than chemo and radiation. I know that you are the true healer and not the doctors.

Touch __(spouse's name)__ and restore his health! Destroy every cancerous cell in his body! Heal anything in his body that has been damaged through the treatments. Dear God, in the name of Jesus, hear my prayer and give my husband's life back! Add good and healthy years to his life. Kill the cancer, and may it never come back. Lastly, Lord, touch __(spouse's name)__ 's mind and give him peace knowing that you are with him, and may your presence bring him comfort.

Thank you, my God, for hearing my prayer. In Jesus's name I place my hope and faith. Amen.

Scripture for Meditation

"Praise the Lord, my soul, and forget not all his benefits—
who forgives all your sins and heals all your diseases"

(Psalm 103:2–3).

Word of Wisdom

God indeed is a miracle worker. It is in Scripture that we have seen Jesus heal diseases. Continue to pray for divine healing knowing that God can heal through medicine, chemo treatments, radiation, or by His divine touch. Hold on to your faith, and never underestimate the power of God. Also trust God during this difficult time. Ultimately it is God's decision to heal, but we also know the power of prayer!

Don't forget to pray for your own strength, and when you feel yourself becoming overwhelmed, talk to a pastor or find a support group in your area where you can find additional strength and support from others who are experiencing the same as you are. Be sure to always lean on God.

31. Mother-in-Law Blues

Gracious and kind, loving God,

I bless your name forever and ever, for you are God of all, and you are worthy of my praise and worship. Therefore I honor you all the days of my life, for I am fully aware not only of your existence but also of your unfailing love.

I come before you, dear God, because my mother-in-law is driving me crazy. I know it's wrong, but I don't like her, God. She interferes in my marriage. She tells lies on me, and she tries to put a wedge between me and my husband. I try so hard to be kind, but she is sneaky and conniving. I don't trust her, Lord, and I know that who she is should not change who I am, but I can't take her disrespect toward me.

My husband doesn't see what I see, and she has a way of making everyone else think that I have a problem with her. Help me, dear Lord. Please show me what to do, and open my husband's eyes to see what is really going on.

And, Lord, help me to still show respect, and help me to still show kindness. Help me, O God, not to allow my anger to get the best of me when I am dealing with my husband's mother.

Thank you, Lord, for always listening to me and helping me to work things out. Thank you, Lord, in Jesus's name.

Scripture for Meditation

"Bless those who curse you, pray for those who mistreat you"

(Luke 6:28).

Word of Wisdom

No one should have to subject him or herself to anyone's abuse or mistreatment. Don't feel compelled to accept the mistreatment or disrespect because it is your mother-in-law. Consider talking to your husband again because it would be more beneficial for him to approach his mother on your behalf. If he will not speak up on your behalf, you may want to consider speaking with your mother-in-law one-on-one and be honest about how she makes you feel.

If your mother-in-law is not willing to acknowledge your feelings, then it is up to you to establish appropriate boundaries. When your mother-in-law begins to make you feel uncomfortable or appears that she is trying to incite some sort of emotion from you, you can walk away or remove yourself from the situation.

Remain respectful, remain prayerful, and choose not to stoop down to your mother-in-law's level. Trust the Lord to be your strength, but refuse to be mistreated.

32. Husband Seems Distant

Magnificent and holy God,

I sing praises unto your name, for you are good and perfect in all your ways. I thank you for this opportunity to come before you to bear my heart and to empty my soul. Lord, I come before you trying to seek understanding as to why my husband seems distant. We don't communicate like we used to. Our marriage seems to lack laughter and joy these days, and our time together seems to have diminished. Even when we are home, he is in one room, and I am in another. And if we are in the same room, the conversation is minimal and surface.

Lord, I don't know what to do. When I ask him if something is wrong, he says nothing. When I try to hold a conversation, I do most of the talking. If I ask him about his day, his response is brief.

Lord, I don't want to begin to make assumptions regarding his distance toward me. I don't know if he is having an affair or is just unhappy. I don't know if he wants out of the marriage, or if there is a problem that he is trying to handle alone. Lord, I just don't know.

Please, dear God, give me patience, but at the same time touch my husband's heart to open up to me. I pray, dear God, that (husband's name) will just let me in and let me know what's wrong. Lord, I put this into your hands. I trust that you will somehow speak to my husband, and if he cannot talk to me quite yet, I pray that he will talk to you.

Thank you, my God, for hearing my prayers, in Jesus's name.

Scripture for Meditation

"Hear my prayer, LORD, listen to my cry for help; do not be deaf to my weeping…"

(Psalm 39:12).

Word of Wisdom

Men tend to keep their feelings and thoughts inside. Do not make the assumption that your husband's silence is in direct relation to his thoughts and feelings about you or the marriage. There may be something troubling him that he isn't comfortable sharing with you at this time. He may be dealing with personal disappointments in his life. Be careful not to badger your husband with questions—that would just make him withdraw even more.

Although he may not be talking much or sharing much, try talking to your husband about different topics and subjects. Seek his advice on an issue, or share your day with him. It may cause him to let his guard down and begin conversation. As he eventually opens up (prayerfully) about things he may be dealing with, rather than trying to fix the problem or telling him how to handle it, just listen and show support. As the communication level increases, begin to talk about the marriage and how much you love him and look forward to your future together.

If over time it seems that nothing works, consider speaking to a professional counselor, who may be able to give you some practical advice in helping to restore the communication in your marriage. Lastly, pray! Pray for your heart not to be hardened but to be patient, and also pray that God will touch your husband's heart to open up to you. Trust that God is with you.

33. Fighting over Finances

Magnificent and holy God,

All honor and glory belongs to you! For you are the one and only living God from whom all life flows. I love you and adore you for being my God, and I am grateful that you allow me to talk to you about anything and everything. Thank you for always listening, and for always giving me what I need.

Once again, I seek your guidance. Once again, I seek your wisdom for my marriage. Our finances are out of order, and it is the source of our arguing and fighting. We just can't seem to be on the same page when it comes to our finances and how the money is to be used. It really seems like we are working against each other rather that working together to resolve our financial problems.

Please, Lord, help us to be in agreement with what the problem is. Help us to work together and to know when to compromise. Help us to manage our finances together, to budget together, and to be on one accord as to how to fix our financial problems.

I pray, O God, that we can both do our part to be faithful with our money and to prioritize together. I also pray that we don't treat our money as my money or his money but rather, our money. I trust that you will help us to resolve our money problems as we seek to do the right things and correct bad financial behaviors.

Thanking you in advance, Lord, for giving us the solu-
tion that we will need to get back on track. I love you with
all my heart. In Jesus's name I pray.

Scripture for Meditation

"Of what use is money in the hand of a fool, since he has
no desire to get wisdom"

(Proverbs 17:16).

Word of Wisdom

Money problems are one of the top causes of divorce. When money problems or surmounting debt occurs, it often creates tension in marriage. It
doesn't matter if the money problems were due to misspending, poor
money management, lost wages from layoff or sickness, or lack of communication about where the money is going because when bills pile up
and money is limited, tension grows. This is why it is important for couples to plan, communicate, and manage their finances together.

However, many couples choose to manage their money separately.
They view their money as mine or yours rather than ours, and so when
problems occur, the finger-pointing and blame begins. Whether you and
your spouse manage your money separately or together, ultimately the
household and marriage will suffer if you are not on one accord and working as a team.

It may be necessary for you and your spouse to at least agree to meet
with a financial planner who can be impartial and who would help you
both to do what is best for the household. Or you may consider attending a budget or financial class in order to get the necessary wisdom and
information for you both to get back on track. Pray for wisdom as to what
the two of you need to do in order to get on the right track financially.

34. Feeling Unloved

God of Heaven,

You are indeed the love of my life. I wouldn't even know love if I had not experienced your love. Your love comforts me. Your love fills me with joy. Your loves makes me feel secure, and it was your love that saved me through your Son, Jesus Christ. I thank you, O God, for perfect love, an unconditional love.

And, Lord, if I can be honest, I want to feel loved in my marriage. I know that no one's love can compare to yours, but I want to feel and know that I am loved by my husband. I want to feel his love by the way he talks to me, treats me, and looks at me. But sometimes, Lord, I wonder if he is still in love with me. I don't feel special to him anymore, and he doesn't look at me the way he used to, with gleam in his eyes.

He doesn't touch me with gentleness and warmth anymore. He doesn't compliment me or speak softly to me. Sometimes I feel like he looks right through me and doesn't even see me anymore. Lord, I don't want to be led by my feelings and emotions. I don't want to make the assumption that he no longer loves me, but I miss the way that he used to make me feel. Maybe I am wanting too much, or maybe this is what happens when you've been married for a while. I don't know, God, but what I do know is how I feel.

Comfort me, my Lord. I need you right now. In Jesus's name I pray. Amen.

Scripture for Meditation

"I am my beloved's, And his desire is for me"

(Song of Solomon 7:10).

"May he kiss me with the kisses of his mouth! For your love is better than wine"

(Song of Solomon 1:2).

Word of Wisdom

We may not always be able to help how we feel, but we must be careful not to make our feelings our truth. Even if your husband doesn't express his love the way that you desire him to, it doesn't mean that he no longer loves you. Unfortunately, sometimes in the midst of marriage we forget how to court, admire, flirt, and speak in our spouse's love language. Sometimes marriage becomes stagnant not because we don't love one another but because we have allowed children, careers, and other things to get in the way.

If you have not done so, consider setting up some special date nights or plan a romantic evening, and show your husband how much he means to you. It is quite possible that your husband may not feel loved either or may feel that you are no longer attracted to him. If it seems that nothing you or he does changes how you feel, pray together for renewal in your marriage. Personal counseling may be a final option for you to discover if there is an unrealized underlying issue to your feelings.

35. To Be More Devoted to My Marriage

My Glorious God,

You are my joy and the lifter of my head. There is truly indeed none like you. You are all that is good and all that is pure. You are love, and you are light; therefore in you there is no darkness and no evil. You are holy and righteous, yet you love those of us who are unholy and unrighteous. In fact you loved us so much that you sent your beloved Son into the world to die for our sins so that we can have an eternal relationship with you. Thank you, my dear God, for unimaginable love.

I call on your name, dear God, because I recognize that I have not been putting my all into my marriage. It's not because of anything that my husband has done, and I am not sure why I have not been fully devoted to my marriage. I love my husband, but I seem to put everything else before him and our marriage. Lord, I don't want my marriage to one day end in divorce or for my husband to become attracted to someone else because I have not given much time and attention to our relationship.

So, Lord, I ask you to help me to make my marriage and husband a priority. Help me, O God, to not allow anyone or anything to stand in the way of me showing my love and commitment to my marriage. Help me, my God, to recognize the covenant that we have together and to honor that covenant and to honor my husband, whom you have brought into my life. I pray that he will begin to feel my love and heart for him and our marriage because I do love my husband although I don't always show it.

Thank you, my dear God, for even bringing it to my attention and awareness that I need to make a change if I want to have a wonderful and lasting marriage. Thank you for being the kind of God that I can be open and honest with. Now, O God, help me to get right.

I love you, my God. In Jesus's name I pray.

Scripture for Meditation

"This is how we know what love is: Jesus Christ laid down his life for us. And we ought to lay down our lives for our brothers and sisters"

(1 John 3:16).

Word of Wisdom

To have a successful marriage it takes time, effort, energy, and devotion from both partners. Marriage is an investment where you can only get out what you are willing to put in. The good thing is that you recognize that you have short-changed your marriage by putting in very little. The good news is you can begin to make a hefty deposit into the relationship beginning now. Look over your schedule, and be willing to sacrifice something on your schedule for the sake of spending some valuable time with your spouse. Of course this cannot be a one-time thing nor should you have to make it a habit of scheduling time for your spouse or marriage. In fact, everything else should revolve around your marriage so that your marriage can be the top priority in your life. It doesn't mean that you cannot have outside friends, a career, personal goals, or hobbies, but it does mean that you are willing to do whatever it takes to help create a loving home and lasting relationship.

36. Better Communication

Most holy God,

Blessed be your holy name for all generations, for you are great and worthy of all praise. Not only, O God, are you clothed with splendor and majesty, but glorious and majestic are your deeds. Your greatness, love, and faithfulness are beyond what my mind can fathom, but thank you for giving me just enough of yourself to be able to praise you and honor you. Thank you for not just being God but for being my God, my Heavenly Father, Abba.

And it is you that I seek because you are the answer to my prayers. You have all power and might to change any situation or to fix any problem. That's why I call on you now, my precious God, because I am crying out for my marriage. I am crying out that my husband and I can be on one accord and in agreement with what's right for us, our marriage, and our home. Sometimes it seems as if we are moving in opposite directions because we don't really communicate like we should.

We need your help, my Lord, because we are not seeing eye to eye because we don't talk first before making plans or decisions that affect our marriage or home. Help us, dear Lord, to realize that we have to work together, but we can't work together if we are not first communicating. My dear God, I don't blame my husband, I blame us. I take responsibility too for decisions that I have made without consulting him first, but now we have to stop the blame game if we want to move forward in our marriage.

So I ask you, Lord, to please help us both to be able to listen and hear, to be able to give and take, and for both of us to make the needed sacrifices for what's best for the marriage.

Thank you, Lord, once again for hearing my prayer. I thank you in Jesus's name. Amen.

Scripture for Meditation

"Pride only breeds quarrels, but wisdom is found in those who take advice"

(Proverbs 13:10).

"The way of fools seems right to them, but the wise listens to advice"

(Proverbs 12:15).

Word of Wisdom

Communication is needed and necessary for any kind of relationship, whether it is husband and wife, parent and child, or even in our relationship with the Lord. Communication keeps us connected and allows for us to not only express our hearts and thoughts but also to hear the heart and thoughts of another.

Marriage without communication is like a road map without street names. It is pointless, ineffective, and useless because you have no idea of where you're going, and so you waste time going somewhere that leads to nowhere. A failure to communicate is an attack on the future of your marriage. Without communication there are no shared goals, plans, and dreams, which leaves you both going in different directions.

Consider finding time for the two of you, possibly over dinner or when you both can have uninterrupted time together, to dream and envision what the future can look like. Both of you can take turns to call out or write down what you would like to see in the marriage and in your future. The only rule is that you cannot criticize the other's remarks or comments. After a list has been completed, one by one discuss how it can be accomplished together. After that has been done, decide on two or three things that you can begin to work toward now.

Another suggestion is to invite your spouse into a conversation by asking him what he thinks on a matter and to be willing to listen and not criticize. For instance, there is a new position available on your job, and you are not sure if you want to apply for it or not. Talk to your spouse about your uncertainty, and then ask him for his thoughts or opinion. Also, listen to your husband when he brings up topics and situations and become engaged in what he is saying. Ask questions. Affirm him. Offer advice only if he asks. Of course these things will not change the relationship overnight, but it is a start to building communication.

37. Husband Dealing with Stress

My Precious Lord,

I glorify your name, for there is no other name that brings me peace and joy. You alone are my strength and my comfort. You bring hope and purpose to my life. I am grateful and thankful for all that you have done for me. For you, O God, have kept me and watched over me. You have always been there even when I was not aware of your presence in my life. Thank you, my God, for loving me and for being a God that I can confide in and share all that's in my heart.

Lord, I come before you lifting my husband up to you. He is so stressed and overwhelmed, and he is beginning to scare me because I don't want him to end up having a heart attack or a breakdown. He seems so frustrated, and I don't know how to help him, Lord. No matter what I say or do, it doesn't seem to help. I can see the heaviness upon him.

Lord, I ask for your peace to fall upon (husband's name). I pray, Lord, that he trusts you and will seek you during this difficult time. Lord, help him not to hold on to things that he cannot change but to seek you for wisdom and guidance. I need you, Lord, to be his strength, just as you are mine. Please, my dear God, show my husband that you do care and that you see what he is going through. Give him what he needs, Lord, and may it be evident to him, Lord, that it was you that came to his side.

I pray that my husband will begin to trust you and know that you are his help. Thank you, my Lord, for hearing and receiving my prayer. In Jesus's name I pray. Amen.

Scripture for Meditation

"Do not be anxious about anything, but in everything, by prayer and petition, with thanksgiving, present your requests to God. And the peace of God, which transcends all understanding, will guard your hearts and your minds in Christ Jesus"

(Philippians 4:6–7).

"Cast all your anxiety on him because he cares for you"

(1 Peter 5:7).

Word of Wisdom

Continue to pray for your husband, and let your husband know that you are worried about him. If his stress is affecting the mood of the house, be honest, and let him know that everyone is affected and worried. Encourage him to talk with a pastor or professional counselor. If he isn't open to talking to someone, continue to do all that you can to offer support, whether emotional support or by offering to help provide assistance in some kind of way to ease the burden.

If the stress is due to hardship, be supportive, and let him know that together the two of you will get through it. If he is frustrated because his efforts seem fruitless, just continue to motivate him to keep trying. Also be sure to not allow his stress to cause you stress. If the stress has been going on for a long time, inform your husband of the toll that it is putting on the marriage and the need for counseling. Lastly, you can schedule your husband a doctor's appointment, and maybe the doctor can direct your husband in finding help that he may need. While you are seeking to be there for your husband, be sure that you continue to lean on God for your own strength as well.

38. Prayer of Blessing over Husband

My Dear God,

Praise and honor belongs to you, for you are so amazing. My words cannot truly express all that you are and all that you mean to me. I am grateful and thankful that you have come into my life and that you love me fully and completely. You are my God, and you continually meet my needs.

I come before you, O God, lifting my husband up to you asking for your hand of blessing to be on him. I ask you, my God, that you protect his life, protect his mind, and protect his health. May no harm or calamity come his way. May his life be filled with peace, love, joy, and happiness. May he feel your presence in his life. May he trust you and depend on you as his God. Dear God, fill him with wisdom that only you can provide. Touch his mind so that he is not worried or fretting over life's problems. Touch his heart so that it may never grow hard or calloused. And touch his spirit, O God, so that his spirit always trusts in your Spirit.

May my husband be respected in the community and honored by those who know him because of his character and integrity. Bless him, my God, and he shall be blessed. I thank you for hearing and answering my prayer. In Jesus's name I pray. Amen.

Scripture for Meditation

"Her husband is respected at the city gate, where he takes
his seat among the elders of the land"

(Proverbs 31:23).

Word of Wisdom

There is power in a praying wife! Continue to keep your husband covered
in prayer. Whether you pray over him directly or pray with him in your personal prayer time, know that God not only hears your prayer but also that
God is indeed with your husband. Also be sure to bless your husband by
your words of affirmation, your respect, love, and loyalty. Your husband
will be empowered by your love and support, which will also help him to
walk in confidence and assurance.

39. Greater Respect for Husband

Dear Heavenly Father,

I thank you for this opportunity to come before you to talk to you openly and honestly without fear of judgment and condemnation. Thank you that I can be myself and be real with you knowing that you are already fully aware of who I am and those things that I struggle with. And that's why I am coming to you, Lord, because I know that I am not right. I know that there are things that I need to change, but I also know that I cannot do it without you. I need your strength and power to help me to be what you desire for me to be.

Lord, I acknowledge that I don't treat my husband well. Sometimes, Lord, I am cruel and mean toward him, and I am not sure why. Sometimes I will cuss him out and will treat him like he doesn't matter. I now recognize, Lord, how wrong I am, and neither my husband nor anyone else deserves to be treated that way. Lord, I repent of my actions, and I seek your forgiveness because I know that I am outside your will and that I am hindering my own blessings in life as well as any kind of relationship with you.

I ask you, O God, to change my heart. Help me to change how I say things and what I say to my husband. Help me to love him the right way. God, I ask you to heal me and to clean me up from the inside out. Save me, and save my marriage, Lord. Heal my husband of any wounds that I may have caused. Heal us, my dear God. In Jesus's name I pray.

Scripture for Meditation

"However, each one of you also must love his wife as he loves himself, and the wife must respect her husband"

(Ephesians 5:33).

Word of Wisdom

It's honorable to recognize pain that you may have caused or are causing along with a desire to change. This is the kind of prayer that God honors! God wants you healed and whole, and the fact that you are able to be mean or cruel to your own husband is a sign that something has gone wrong in your life or heart. The good news is that God specializes in people like you—people who are open and honest about their need for repentance, healing, or deliverance.

I encourage you to continue to pray but to pray each day asking God to help you speak words of life and affirmation to your husband. Ask God to help you to guard your tongue and to be cautious of not only what you say to your husband but also of your actions and mannerisms toward your husband. If you do not attend a church, consider finding a church where you can grow closer to God so that you may receive the spiritual teaching, support, and accountability that you need. If you recognize any unresolved hurt in your life that may be the driving factor of your negative behavior toward your husband, consider meeting with a pastor or spiritual counselor for additional assistance toward healing.

Lastly, share with your husband that you acknowledge that you have not shown him the love and respect he deserves and that you are seeking God in helping you to change. Seek forgiveness from your husband, and let him know that despite the things that you have done and said to him, you really do love him, and you want your marriage to work.

40. Financial Blessing for Our Home

Gracious and loving God,

I bless your name forever and ever, for in your name there is peace and joy. Your name is my strength and my comfort. I call on your name because you are my rock and my refuge. In you, O God, is life, and I love the life that you have given me through your Son and my Savior, Jesus Christ.

Because you are my God, I depend on you for my every need. Your word teaches me that you already know what I am in need of, and therefore I have no need to worry. I thank you, my God, that you have always taken care of my family's needs, but, Lord, I ask you now for a financial blessing for our home. I ask you, O God, to relieve us of our financial strain. It seems that we just can't get our head above water. Even when we manage to meet our financial needs, something comes up that costs us more money and then sets us back once again.

Lord, we have very little savings. We can't get things fixed around the house. We have not taken a vacation in a long time. I come to you, O God, because you have the power to bless us. You have the power to increase our finances. You have the power, my God, to give us more than what we need so that we can not only pay our bills but also save money and enjoy some things in life.

Lord, I come before you with a humble spirit, not seeking to get rich, not seeking material gain in which to brag or boast. I would just love for my husband and me to be able to have some financial relief because we never seem to have it. Search my heart, Lord, and know that my motives and desires are pure. I thank you, my Lord, for hearing my prayer and for blessing my home with all that is good. I thank you for the financial blessing that is on the way. I love and adore you, my God. It is in Jesus's name that I offer this prayer. Amen.

Scripture Reference

"Therefore I tell you, do not worry about your life, what you will eat or drink; or about your body, what you will wear. Is not life more than food, and the body more than clothes? Look at the birds of the air; they do not sow or reap or store away in barns, and yet your Heavenly Father feeds them. Are you not much more valuable than they? Can any one of you by worrying add a single hour to your life?…But seek first his kingdom and his righteousness, and all these things will be given to you as well"

(Matthew 6:25–27, 33).

Word of Wisdom

Trust and believe in the power of God to improve your financial situation. Be sure that there is no reckless spending from either you or your husband. If you and your husband are doing everything that you know to do, pray together for God's blessings to fill every area of your life. Also know that there is nothing wrong with wanting to go on a vacation or to enjoy some things in life. Continue to walk by faith, and wait with anticipation for the blessing that God will pour into your life. God is able!

~ Chapter Three ~

Prayers for Singles

*An unmarried woman is concerned about the
Lord's affairs...*

—1 Corinthians 7:34

*Being single doesn't mean that you know nothing
about love.
Sometimes being solo is wiser than being in a false
relationship.*

—Unknown

41. Longing for Marriage

My glorious God,

I bless your name and honor you as God of all. I also honor you as the one who gave me life and keeps me each and every day. I am grateful and thankful that you are always with me and therefore I am not alone.

But, Lord, I feel so lonely. Not because you are not in my life but because I really want to be married. I really want a special person to share my life with. I want someone to come home to everyday, someone to snuggle with, share laughs with, and talk to.

I don't want just anyone but someone who can love me for who I really am and whom I can love for who he really is. I want someone who will treat me like a queen and whom I can treat as a king. I want someone who can make me laugh and whom I can make happy because we seem made for each other. I ask you, Lord, to please hear my prayer and send that person who you approve of into my life. God, you know what I like and what I need, so I will trust you, O God, for that special person designed just for me.

In the meantime please help me to be patient and not to settle for anything less than your best for me. Please give me wisdom and discernment to see beyond a person's exterior to really see what is in his heart. Lord, may I not become distracted by the longing of a relationship but instead enjoy my life and fulfill your will as I wait on that special someone that you have for me.

Thank you, Lord, that I can talk to you about anything!
I pray this prayer in your Son Jesus's name.

Scripture for Meditation

"But if we hope for what we do not yet have, we wait for
it patiently"

(Romans 8:25).

Word of Wisdom

Whatever we ask of God, God is able to provide. Just be sure to not have
unrealistic expectations of the perfect man, who does not exist. However,
it may be wise to have a list of negotiable and nonnegotiable attributes
when you do meet a potential life partner. What areas are you willing
to compromise? For instance, does the person have to be the specific
height that you like? Do they have to be as educated as you or make a
certain amount of money? An example of a nonnegotiable condition is
the requirement for him to believe in Jesus Christ as his Savior or that he
must desire children because you desire children.

Once you have your negotiable and nonnegotiable conditions in
place, continue to move forward with your life. Trust that God can connect you and your future spouse in the right place at just the right time.
Also know that God does not always respond as quickly as we would like.
Therefore be patient, enjoy life, pursue your dreams, and discover God's
will for your life at this time.

42. Overcoming Promiscuity

O Merciful God,

I come to you as the God of my life. You created me, and I know that I am here for your purpose. I know that you have a will and desire for my life, but I also know that much of the time I don't live up to it.

Lord, I know that it is not your will for me to live a promiscuous life. I know that you have something better planned for me. Yet, I continue to enter into these sexual relationships with different people. I don't know why I do this, Lord. I don't even feel good about it. Most of the time I feel empty afterward, but for whatever reason, I don't stop.

I have had one-night stands. I have slept with married men, and I am not proud of any of it. Lord, I know that I am not telling you anything that you don't already know, but I am coming to you because I need the strength to walk away from this lifestyle.

I need you, dear Lord, to deliver me from this bondage. I know that my lifestyle breaks your heart, and it breaks my heart knowing that my poor choices hurt you. Do know that I want to live right. I want to stop sleeping around. I want to take control of my body and my actions, so, Lord, I ask you to give me strength for today. Help me, my God, to love me too much to not protect and honor my own body.

Help me to change my focus and nurture my relationship with you. Show me what you have for me that's better than the life I am now living.

Thank you, Lord, for not turning your back on me and for loving me. And I thank you that you will be my strength to get my life together. In the name of Jesus Christ, my Savior, I pray.

Scripture for Meditation

"Flee from sexual immorality. All other sins a person commits are outside the body, but whoever sins sexually, sins against their own body. Do you not know that your bodies are temples of the Holy Spirit, who is in you, whom you have received from God? You are not your own; you were bought at a price. Therefore honor God with your bodies"

(1 Corinthians 6:18–20).

Word of Wisdom

In a situation such as this, you not only need to pray for deliverance, but you may also need to do some self-reflection. What is the root cause of the behavior? Is it loneliness, poor self-esteem, or the desire to be loved and wanted? So many things can be the root cause of your actions, but even if you do not know the answer as to why, know that God can help you to overcome this behavior. However, God needs your participation—you must be willing to put some boundaries in place.

For instance, refuse to accept sexual advances from married men. Don't accept their phone number, and don't even flirt back. Another thing that you can do is to make a decision not to date for a while, and focus on your relationship with God. Abstain from men for some time by taking a hiatus from dating.

Because your sexual behavior has been a part of your life for some time, I suggest that you pray daily. Each day ask God to help you to make wise decisions for today according to his will. As you seek God, you will begin to feel God's strength and presence in your life.

I also encourage you to find an accountability partner or talk with your pastor. Whomever you choose to be accountable with, it needs to be someone who is living the life that you desire to live but is also nonjudgmental. In the meantime keep praying. Keep trusting God. Keep boundaries in place. Fight for your deliverance one day at a time and one decision at a time. You can overcome this lifestyle with the power of God.

43. Strength to Walk Away from Unhappy Relationship

Dear God,

Honor and glory belong to you. You are a holy God and perfect in all your ways. I praise you because there is no one like you. Thank you for your perfect love and your compassion, which never fails. Thank you that each day is a fresh start and a new beginning in which to know you better and live life better and more wisely.

I come to you, my God, because I need your guidance and power. I can't seem to walk away from this relationship. Lord, this relationship is dysfunctional, and it doesn't seem to be getting any better. I know that we are not married, so I should be able to just walk away, but obviously I can't. No matter what he does, I just continue to forgive him. I know that I am not perfect either because of my own flaws. In fact I don't believe that we are good for each other.

Help me, Lord, to get my life on the right track and not to stay in a relationship that isn't going anywhere. I love him, Lord, but help me to realize that I need to love myself more and not settle for this dysfunctional relationship.

In Jesus's name I pray.

Scripture for Meditation

"Since we have these promises, dear friends, let us purify ourselves from everything that contaminates body and spirit, perfecting holiness out of reverence for God"

(2 Corinthians 7:1).

Word of Wisdom

Of course if it were easy for you to walk away, you would have walked away by now. The question that you must ask yourself is, "Am I worth more than what I am getting?" If the relationship does not enhance, improve, or add any value to your life, why are you hanging on to it? Is there fear of being alone? Have you grown dependent on this person?

You must make up in your mind that this relationship is not what you want and then walk away. You must believe that freedom, peace, joy, and happiness is on the other side of the door, but you won't experience them until you actually walk through that door. Pray daily for God's strength and power to do what you know leads to your peace and freedom. You've got more power than you think.

44. Single Parenting Prayer

Holy and magnificent God,

Who is like you—majestic in holiness and awesome in glory! You alone reign supreme, and you alone hold all things together. The depth of your love is beyond comprehension, but I thank you that you have demonstrated your love for us through the sacrifice and death of your Son so that we may be saved. Thank you, Lord God, for a love that cannot be earned because you love us with a perfect love. Thank you for revealing yourself to me because I cannot imagine life without you.

I know, Lord, that you are with me, but I need you even more, O God, as I struggle to raise my children. I need you, my God, to help me to provide for my children's needs. Please, Lord, give me what I need so that my children have clothes, food, a roof over their head, and a safe environment. I even need emotional support, Lord, because sometimes I get so tired of having to do this alone.

I ask, Lord, that you keep me strong and help me to continue to provide a loving and happy home for my children. Help me to believe that it is possible even as a single mother to raise God-fearing children who will one day live productive lives. Help me not to see myself as deficient in any way. Help me not to envy those households where there are two loving parents. Help me, Lord, to see myself whole, complete, equipped, and perfectly capable of raising my children. May I be reminded daily that I am not alone because you are with me and that what is really important is a loving and God-filled home.

Thanks, Lord. In Jesus's name I pray.

Scripture for Meditation

"I instruct you in the way of wisdom and lead you along straight paths"

(Proverbs 4:11).

Word of Wisdom

Know that as a single mother you are not deficient in any way. Believe that God has given you everything that you need to raise your children and to provide for their physical and emotional needs. Consider searching for a single mothers group, in which you can get support and have relationships with other single mothers. When possible, be sure to make time for yourself to clear your head and get a moment of rest. It is okay to step away for a moment to refresh. Lastly, it takes a village to raise a child. Be sure to include family and friends in your life who may be able to offer you and the children the necessary support.

45. Financial Stability

Dear Father in Heaven,

Bless your name! You are deserving of all praise and honor. You are a holy and righteous God, and in you there is no darkness. Your ways are not our ways, and you act in accordance to your will and purpose. I am so thankful and grateful for your love, for your love keeps me and comforts me. Your love gives me the strength to endure. And because I know that you love me, I know that you are always with me.

But, Lord, I need you once again. I just can't seem to find financial relief. I just don't have enough money coming in to help cover my bills. Honestly, dear God, I just don't make enough money to cover some of the basic things that I need in life without financial strain.

Please, God, help me to overcome my financial problems. I need a better income, a financial blessing, or just a new job. I know that you are able to help me to overcome my financial problems, for you are a God who is more than able to supply all of my needs. Therefore, I put my hope and faith in you. Thank you, Lord, for hearing my prayers.

In the name of Jesus I pray. Amen.

Scripture for Meditation

"Ask and it will be given to you; seek and you will find; knock and the door will be opened to you. For everyone who asks receives; he who seeks finds; and to him who knocks, the door will be opened"

(Matthew 7:7–8).

Word of Wisdom

God is a miracle-working God. Nothing that we ask of God is impossible. However, you may need to assess whether or not your current job provides the opportunity that you need for advancement or greater wages. If so, how often are job openings available? If not, is it time for you to find another place of employment? If your job search is bringing forth no results, pray fervently that God will make your resume stand out and that you will gain favor with the interviewer. You may also have to consider whether or not you need to secure a second job until the job that you desire comes through. Keep praying, for God does work miracles, but also remain active for doors that God may open in your life for a more financially secure future.

46. Freedom to Enjoy Life

My God,

There are no words to express your greatness, for your greatness no one can fathom. You perform countless miracles. You give life and sustain life. You are slow to anger and abounding in love. Who is like you, O God? You are indeed worthy of all praise! I honor you as my God who gives me hope and secures my future. Thank you for loving me with a matchless love. Thank you for watching over me and never leaving me alone. You are my confidence and strength.

I come before you, Lord, just seeking to be free in life. Help me to not take life so seriously that I cannot enjoy my life or find ways to have fun. I don't know why it is hard for me to relax and to let my hair down, but I don't want life to pass me by, and I never do anything simply for enjoyment. Lord, of course I don't want to live recklessly, but I don't want to live so cautiously that I fail to find laughter and enjoyment in my life.

Please help me to relax, O Lord, and to know that it's okay to enjoy the life that you alone blessed me with. Help me to realize that you desire to fill my life with good things, which include laughter and fun. Help me, my dear God, to know that it is okay to break from the grind and work for rest and occasional fun. Thank you, my Lord, for hearing my prayers in the precious name of my Lord and Savior, Jesus Christ.

Scripture for Meditation

"…I have come that they may have life, and have it to the full"

(John 10:10).

Word of Wisdom

Life is filled with so much pain and tragedy that when we have the opportunity to escape and be free for a moment to laugh and enjoy life, we have to take advantage of it! If your lack of fun is simply because you don't know how to have fun, put together a bucket list of things that you would like to do. Check your local newspaper to see what exciting things may be going on in your town. Attend a concert, an art fair, a new restaurant with some friends, or even possibly go to a comedy show for some laughs. If you work hard every day and are faithful to your responsibilities, don't you think you deserve to have a little fun mixed in?

47. Depression

My Father in Heaven,

You are my strength and my reason for being. You are my God, and you give me hope for a better tomorrow. I stand on your promises for my life believing, dear God, that what you have in store for me is beyond what my mind can fathom. You are a good God, and your love fills me, yet I find myself in darkness. I know that you are real and you keep me holding on, but I need your light right now, O God, to chase away this darkness that I am in.

Lift the cloud that hangs over my head, dear Lord. Lift my spirit from despair. Lift me from this dark place. Clear my mind of these negative thoughts. Help me to feel what I know to be true. I know that you are here with me. I know that I am not alone. I know that you care for me. I know that you have a purpose for my life. I know that you are my strength, yet I can't shake this heaviness and fog. Deliver me, O Lord. Rescue me from these feelings. Set me free from this prison. Shine your light on me. Hold me close, and don't let me go. Keep your arms wrapped around me. I surrender my soul to you in Jesus's name.

Scripture for Meditation

"The Spirit of the Sovereign Lord is on me, because the Lord has anointed me...to bind up the brokenhearted, to proclaim freedom for the captives and release from darkness for the prisoners...comfort all who mourn...to bestow on them a crown of beauty instead of ashes, the oil of gladness instead of mourning, and a garment of praise instead of a spirit of despair..."

(Isaiah 61:1-10).

Word of Wisdom

It is great that you acknowledge your depression and understand the need to open up to God. Talking to God can be very therapeutic and comforting for your soul. Never be afraid to express your heart to God and seek his comfort and strength. If you are in a season of depression due to circumstances, find someone that you can talk to who can also pray with you. Remember as well to saturate your mind with God's promises. Trust that God is going to get your through this difficult time that you are now in.

If you suffer from clinical or seasonal depression, it is good that you are praying to God, but also follow the advice and counsel of your therapist or doctor. God sometimes heals supernaturally and at other times God heals through medication. If you have a pastor, consider meeting with your pastor for spiritual support in addition to any other counseling that you may be receiving.

Lastly, never feel ashamed about your depression. Trust God even in the darkness. Pray to God. Welcome God's presence in the midst of this battle, and do whatever it takes to live the life that God has called for you, even if it requires medication and therapy. You are not alone. God is with you, and all of Heaven is cheering you on!

48. Spiritual Friendships

God of Heaven and all creation,

Glory and honor belong to you, for you are the eternal, immortal, invisible, and wise God. You, O Lord, are slow to anger and abounding in love. You take delight in all who trust you. You are my joy, for in you there is life and all that is good.

I thank you for becoming real to me. I thank you for opening my eyes to truly see you. I give you praise because you have been good to me. I am eternally grateful and thankful for the many things that you have done in my life especially in saving my soul through your Son, Jesus Christ. May I receive every blessing that is possible through Christ Jesus.

I come before you, my God, asking for spiritual friends. I really need some new people in my life who are seeking to go in the same direction that I am going in. I love my old friends, but I don't want to continue to stumble and make bad choices along with them. Please, dear Lord, put the right people in my path that I can connect with, people who love you and will be good for my spiritual journey as I grow in you. I thank you, Lord, for hearing my prayer, and I thank you for my new relationship with you and the new relationships that you will bring into my life. Love you, and in Jesus's name I pray.

Scripture for Meditation

"The righteous choose their friends carefully, but the way
of the wicked leads them astray"

(Proverbs 12:26).

Word of Wisdom

The right friendships are very important on your spiritual journey with Christ. Not only do we need God, but we also need others as well for added strength, encouragement, support, and wisdom. Because our spiritual walk is not an easy walk, the right people in your life can help keep you motivated, and you can also help keep them motivated in their times of trouble or weakness.

If you belong to a church, I encourage you to find ways to get involved. Serving in your church will help you to connect to new people and possibly make new friendships. Also be sure to keep God in the process of finding the right friendships. Not everyone in church is in a healthy place, and therefore you want to be connected to the right person—someone who is compatible with you considering where you are on your journey.

49. The Need to Love Myself

Dear Heavenly Father,

I bless your holy name. I give you honor and praise for all the marvelous things that you have done. You perform miracles each and every day. You are a God of compassion, who saves those in distress and heals those who are afflicted. You are a merciful God, who gives us chance after chance. Thank you for not giving up on us and for sending your Son to die for us so that we might be saved. Thank you for being the kind of God that you are, a God who is faithful, dependable, and trustworthy. Thank you for being my God.

I come before you, dear Lord, asking you to teach me how to love myself. For so long I have neglected my own needs by trying to be what everyone else wants me to be. I have been mistreated, misused, and taken for granted, and it seems that I am always the one left with the short end of the stick. Show me what love is, and show me how to love myself. Help me not to feel guilty for putting my needs first. Show me that it is okay to do nice things for me.

Help me, O God, to never again be in bondage or dependent of other people's love to determine my value. Help me, dear Lord, not to accept just any kind of ill behavior from anyone because I think that I am not worthy of better. Lift my head, Lord. Give me the confidence and assurance that I need to recognize how wonderful and great I am because I am your daughter. Teach me to love myself so that I won't allow anyone to mistreat me or to take my kindness for weakness. I thank you, my Father, for hearing my prayers and for giving me the confidence that I need. I love you, Lord. In Jesus's name I pray. Amen.

Scripture for Meditation

"But you, LORD, are a shield around me, my glory, the One who lifts my head high"

(Psalm 3:3).

Word of Wisdom

The first step in loving yourself is to affirm who you are in Christ. You are God's daughter, and God created you with purpose. You have been created in God's image and likeness. You are fearfully and wonderfully made. God loved you so much that he allowed his Son to die for you. God cares for you, protects you, forgives you, comforts you, and meets all of your needs. If your Father in Heaven treats you so amazingly, how can you want anything less from anyone else? Of course no one is perfect, but when you love yourself the way God loves you, it becomes impossible to accept disrespectful behavior from anyone.

Loving yourself means to not subject yourself to any form of abuse, mistreatment, or manipulation. Loving yourself is to take care of your spirit, your mind, your body, and your overall well-being. It is not selfish whatsoever. In fact, you won't be able to truly love others until you understand what love is through Christ and how to walk in that love.

50. Faith to Pursue My Dream

My Dear God,

Savior of my soul, lifter of my head, and giver of life, I give you praise and honor as the one and only true God. You are the eternal God and the God of endless love. Your compassion fails not. Your mercies know no limit. Your greatness no one can fathom, and your glory fills the earth. You are the God whom I worship, the God whom I call on, the God whom I trust, for you are the God who has given me life.

I thank you for your constant presence in my life. I thank you for watching over me and keeping me all the days of my life. I thank you that there is never a moment when I am alone. Thank you for loving me.

I ask you, O Lord, to increase my faith. Give me faith to pursue my dreams. Give me the confidence that I need, knowing that you are with me. Help me to overcome the fear of failing. Help me to keep my eyes on you and not the obstacles. Help me, dear Lord, to focus on the vision that you have given me in order to direct my steps. May I trust you to not steer me wrong. May I know that you have already paved the way for me. Give me the courage that I need to move forward so that I won't one day live in regret because I was too fearful to trust you.

Thank you, my Lord, for hearing my prayer and for giving me what I need to pursue what I believe you have placed in my heart. It is in the name of my Lord and Savior that I pray.

Scripture for Meditation

"I took you from the ends of the earth, from its farthest corners I called you. I said, 'You are my servant'; I have chosen you and have not rejected you. So do not fear, for I am with you; do not be dismayed, for I am your God"

(Isaiah 41:9–10).

Word of Wisdom

God gives us dreams and visions to direct our path. The only way for a dream to become a reality is for us to pursue the dream. If you know that God is with you, then you must trust God every step of the way to give you what you need when you need it. To not pursue your dream is to fail—it is to have more faith in failure than in success.

Faith does not necessarily mean the absence of fear, but what it does mean is that despite my fear I will press toward what God has for me. Go ahead and take the second step toward pursuing your dream. You've already taken the first step by praying. The rest is up to you. With God you can do it!

51. Relationship with a Married Man

My dear God,

I come before you crying out to you, seeking forgiveness and mercy. Forgive me for this relationship that I am in with a married man. I know that it isn't your will, and I know that I am hurting you. I knew that it was wrong when he and I became involved, but I was lonely, and I desired him as much as he desired me. Despite the guilt, I continued the relationship, knowing that he has a wife and that I was breaking your heart.

I ask you, dear Lord, to please give me the strength to walk away simply because it goes against your will. Give me the strength to never go back but also the desire to walk away. I know it is wrong, but my heart is so caught up in this relationship. I pray that I do not allow my feelings or my will to supersede your word and your will for my life.

May I be able to hold my head up again and find favor in your sight because I did what was right in your eyes. Thank you for hearing my prayer, O God, and may I not continue in this sinful affair. In humility I pray in Jesus's name. Amen.

Scripture for Meditation

"You have heard that it was said, 'You shall not commit adultery'"

(Matthew 5:27).

Word of Wisdom

You deserve so much more in your life. You deserve to be loved fully and completely by someone who can give himself completely to you. A married man can only give you a small portion of himself because he belongs to someone else. This relationship requires you to hide, keep secrets, and live in falsehood. No matter what he tells you, it is wrong. Not only are you helping him to betray his covenant relationship with his wife, but you are also hurting your own relationship with God.

God's word must have greater power than your desires. Adultery is wrong no matter the reason used to justify it. Don't neglect your relationship with God with something that is temporary and built upon falsehood and deceit. Also, don't trust a man with your heart when it is obvious that he is trampling on his own wife's heart. Do what is right. Walk away. Believe that God can send someone special in your life, someone with whom you can build a relationship free of lies and hiding. Remember, you deserve much more than what you are getting.

52. Healing of Broken Heart (Relationship Ended)

My Lord,

This hurts so bad. I really thought that __(ex-boyfriend's name)__ was the one for me. I really believed that he was the answer to my prayers. I thought, O God, that you sent him to me because he was everything that I needed and wanted.

God, I am so devastated right now. My heart hurts. I am trying to understand what's wrong with me. Why didn't he love me the way that I loved him? What went wrong? Help me to understand this and to make sense of this. I feel like I have invested my time and energy into something that wasn't meant to be.

My God, I feel like such a fool. I have given him my heart. I have shared my dreams. I let my guard down because I was certain that we had a future together. Please, Lord, take this pain away from me. This hurts too much.

Scripture for Meditation

"Trust in the Lord with all your heart and lean not to your own understanding; in all your ways acknowledge him, and he will make your paths straight"

(Proverbs 3:5–6).

Word of Wisdom

When we are dealing with a broken heart, it feels like the pain will never go away and that life will never get back to normal. But the truth is, eventually we heal, we meet new people, and new memories replace the old ones. Although the pain is real, see this as the ending of a chapter in your life, and look forward to the next chapter that will be filled with wonderful surprises. Trust God, heal from the pain, invite God into the process, and continue with living until God really sends that special someone into your life.

53. Desire for Children

My glorious God,

Glory and honor belong to you, for you reign supreme, and there is no one greater than you. You are not only great, but you are worthy of all praise because you give us life, and you give us purpose for living. I thank you, my God, for showing me that you are real. Thank you for opening my eyes to truth to know that you love me and sent your Son to die for me. Thank you for always being there for me, especially when I did not know that you were there. You are good to me, and I am eternally grateful.

Lord, if I can be honest, my heart grieves. I so desire to have a child, a baby from my womb whom I can love and raise. How long, O Lord, must I wait for you to send me someone to love and marry so that we can build a family? Help me, Lord, with this longing that continues to grow as I see others with their children. I am trying to be patient. I am trying to refocus my attention elsewhere, but, Lord, I am not getting younger.

Also, God, I want to do things right in your eyes. I don't want to have a child outside of marriage. I want a father in the home. But, God, I need your help. I need you to make it happen. In the meantime, dear God, help me to be even more patient, as I trust your will to be done in my life. I love you, Lord, and I know that you love me too. Thank you for hearing my heart. In Jesus's name I pray. Amen.

Scripture for Meditation

"Children are a heritage from the Lord, offspring a reward from him"

(Psalm 127:3).

"Therefore I tell you, whatever you ask for in prayer, believe that you have received it, and it will be yours"

(Mark 11:24).

Word of Wisdom

Children are indeed a gift from the Lord, and without children humanity would cease to exist. Unfortunately not everyone can have children, whether it is due to fertility problems, age, lack of a suitable partner, or other. Whatever the reason is for not being able to have children, be sure to never take it personal, as if something were wrong with you or that God didn't want you to have children. In an imperfect world, things don't always go as planned, including getting married or having children.

However, if you are still young or at childbearing age, don't lose hope. God is able! Maybe this just isn't your time, and you need to be a little more patient. If you are growing older or time is against you, adoption is a possibility. Does it replace the need to have your own children? Of course not, but an adopted child could be a blessing to you, and you can be a blessing to that child. If adoption is not an option, seek to continue to live your life and discover what God may have for your future if it does not include children.

Lastly, continue to pray for God. Ask God for peace and to give you the strength or patience that you need, as you walk by faith. Don't lose hope!

54. Faith to Start Over in a New City

Merciful and gracious God,

I come before you as your daughter, seeking you as Lord of my life. I surrender to you as my God and the one whom I look to for answers, direction, and guidance. I acknowledge that I need you more and more each day and that I cannot walk this spiritual journey alone. I am thankful that you are with me every step of the way and that I don't have to fear being alone even when I feel alone. I trust that you are with me and will never leave me or forsake me.

I seek you, dear God, because I need stronger faith. I want to leave where I am and start a new life in a new city, but I am so afraid. I am afraid of the unknown and not knowing what life will be like and what kind of people I will meet. I know that you have not given me a spirit of fear, and deep in my heart, I know that you are with me, but yet, my God, I'm afraid.

Help me, O Lord, to press through the fear. Help me to have the faith that I need, knowing that you have already prepared the way for me and that you have already set things in motion. Help me to feel confident about my decision and to just do it. Lord, I don't want to wake up one day filled with regrets because I didn't have the faith to leave this place.

So, God, by faith, I will start packing. I will start looking for a new place to live. I will begin a job search. I will begin planning my future in a new city. I look forward, dear God, to our relationship growing even more as I step out on faith trusting you to lead the way. It is in Jesus's name that I pray. Amen.

Scripture for Meditation

"For I am the Lord, your God, who takes hold of your right hand and says to you, 'Do not fear; I will help you'"

(Isaiah 41:13).

Word of Wisdom

Faith does not mean the absence of fear. Faith means that despite what I see and how I feel, I will trust God. Of course it is scary starting over and moving to a new city, but it is also exciting! Think about the wonderful people you may meet and the new experiences that await you!

Press through the fear by doing your part to set things in motion, as you believe that God has truly indeed gone ahead of you. Look forward to what the future holds. Live without any regrets, and stand in awe of God while God continues to reveal himself to you as you embark on a new journey. You only live once (in this life), so make the most of it!

~ Chapter Four ~

Prayers for Healing

He heals the brokenhearted and binds up their wounds.

—Psalm 147:3

*The practice of forgiveness is our most important
contribution
to the healing of the world.*

—Marianne Williamson

55. Healing from Divorce

Dear God,

My heart cries out to you. I never wanted to be in this place. I didn't get married, Lord, to be divorced. My marriage was not supposed to end like this. We took vows and pledged our lives together. We promised to stay together no matter what. But here I am, Lord, alone, broken, and hurting.

Why, God, couldn't my marriage end happily ever after? Why did my marriage have to fail? Why did I have to invest so much time and energy into something that would not last?

Help me, Lord, because it hurts so bad. Help me to accept what I don't want to accept. Help me to not have a pity party, not to become bitter, and not to stay stuck in this pain. Help me, O God, because right now I can't do this by myself. I just don't have the strength, and I can't keep trying to fake like I am okay when I am not.

Be my strength, Lord, and my comfort. Be my light in this dark place. May your love empower me to keep moving on. Thank you, Lord, for being what I need and for not leaving me alone. I bless your name forever. In Jesus's name. Amen

Michele Teague-Humphrey

Scripture for Meditation

"The LORD is my strength and my shield; my heart trusts in him, and he helps me"

(Psalm 28:7).

Word of Wisdom

The pain of divorce can be unbearable regardless of the reason for which the marriage ended. It not only leaves a hole in your heart, but it also alters the course of your life. Everything changes after a divorce, and now you have to develop a new normal, in which you develop a new routine.

How long you have been married may determine how long it takes to heal. Do know that healing will not come overnight, but also know that it doesn't have to take a lifetime. If possible try and find a support group for divorcees. Also seek to meet with a pastor for spiritual support through the healing process. What is very important is that you process your emotions, refuse to keep anything bottled in, cry out to God if you have to, and allow healing to take its course. Know that divorce is not the end of your life. Your future still awaits you. In the meantime seek comfort from God.

126

56. Healing from Guilt of Abortion

Dear loving and merciful God,

I thank you that you are indeed a loving and merciful God. I thank you that you love me with unconditional love. I praise you because there is truly no one like you. I don't know, Lord, how you can love me the way that you do. I know that I have broken your heart and disappointed you many times. Yet, you continue to forgive me and continue to show kindness toward me.

But, God, I need your forgiveness again. I know that you have already forgiven me for the abortion, but I can't let go of the guilt and sorrow. My heart is so heavy, and I feel so condemned. I know it wasn't the right thing to do, but I did it anyway.

Merciful God, help me to forgive myself. Help me to not walk in self-condemnation. Help me to heal from the pain. Help me, O God, never to find myself in this same situation again.

Please forgive me, O God, and if you have already forgiven me, help me to forgive myself. Please, God, in Jesus's name.

Scripture for Meditation

"The LORD has heard my cry for mercy; the LORD accepts my prayer"

(Psalm 6:9).

Word of Wisdom

Sometimes the hardest person to forgive is ourselves. We always think that we could have done better, should have done better, or should have been smarter or wiser. Unfortunately in life we make many mistakes, some intentional and some unintentional. Some of those mistakes have helped shape and develop who we are today. Some taught us life lessons, and others took us down a road that we vowed never to travel again.

You had an abortion. You must accept this fact and learn to live with it. However, living with it does not mean that you beat yourself up every day. It doesn't mean that you bow your head in shame. It doesn't mean that you carry it around like an old duffle bag. It begins by trusting and knowing that God has forgiven you, and now you must forgive yourself. But even in forgiving yourself, it takes time to heal emotionally, and although you may never forget the abortion, let it be a reminder of God's grace and mercy during a difficult time of your life. So continue to pray to God. It's okay to grieve, but be sure to seek God's comfort. Rely on God's strength. Walk in God's grace. Trust God to comfort your soul.

57. Healing from Rape

My God,

I never thought this could happen to me. Why me, O God? What did I do to deserve this? Please help me to understand how could something so tragic happen to me? What did I do wrong, Lord? Am I being punished for something? Why didn't you save me? You could have protected me.

Please, Lord, take this pain away. Take the shame away. Take the memory away. Make me forget that this ever happened. Rewind the clock so that I can be in a different place at a different time and avoid that horrific moment.

Help me get through this, O God, or I won't be able to go on. Heal the pain so that I can live again. Be my strength, dear God. Be my hiding place from the world. Keep me in your arms of safety forever, God. In Jesus's name.

Scripture for Meditation

"He gives strength to the weary and increases the power of the weak"

(Isaiah 40:29).

Word of Wisdom

No one deserves to be raped. What happened to you is tragic, and it should have never happened, but you can get through this with counseling, spiritual guidance, and a good support group and system. This is not a situation that you try and handle on your own. You need God and the support of others who love you and who are willing to walk with you through the healing process.

Try not to blame yourself for the evil act of another. Try not to understand why it happened. We live in a fallen world, and oftentimes we are left with no answers in the face of tragedy. Rather than continuously looking back and trying to figure out what you could have done differently or if you had been in a different place, instead look to God for comfort, strength, and healing.

I encourage you if you have not already done so to contact the Rape Crisis Center 24-7 crisis hotline at 210-349-7273. Whether or not the rape was reported to the police, you need all of the support and love that you can get. You may never forget the pain, but God's power can help you to live again.

58. Healing from Disease or Illness

My glorious God,

I call on you, God, because you have created me. You have given me life, and it is you who sustains me each and every day. You created me for your purpose, and you have guided my path in accordance to your will. But now, O God, I need you to touch and heal my body so that I can continue on this journey. I need you, O God, to restore my health and my strength. Dear God, I know that you have the power to heal my body. You can do what doctors and medication cannot always do. You can put me back on my feet again and make me strong once again.

In the name of Jesus, touch this sickness that has infiltrated my body so that it is no more. Breathe on me so that I can be healed inside and out. May your healing power flow through every part of my body and cleanse it from all that weakens me and seeks to rob me of my health. In the name of Jesus, I am healed and made whole by the power of your word and by the name of Jesus in which sickness must flee. Amen.

Scripture for Meditation

"Praise the Lord, O my soul, and forget not all his benefits—who forgives all your sins and heals all your diseases"

(Psalm 103:2–3).

Word of Wisdom

In the midst of following doctor's orders and doing your part to get healthy, continue to call on the name of the Lord for your healing. God heals through medicine, surgery, therapy, and diet, but God also heals supernaturally! Never underestimate the power of God, and while you are praying for divine healing, ask God to fill you with his peace and to surround you with his love. Trust God in the midst of your sickness, and know that God is with you.

59. Healing from Betrayal of Trust from a Friend

Dear Lord,

I bless your name. I am so grateful and thankful that you are not like us. I thank you for your unconditional love and the fact that you are no respecter of persons—you love us all the same—and I thank you for that. Because of that I know that I can trust you, call on you, depend on you, and even cry out to you, and you will always be there for me. Thank you for your faithfulness to me even when I am not as faithful as I need to be.

Lord, I know that I am not perfect, and I have done things to hurt others, but, Lord, I feel so betrayed right now by ___(person's name)___. I can't believe what he/she did to me. Friends are supposed to be there for one another and have each other's back, but ___(person's name)___ has treated me more like an enemy than a friend.

God, I need your strength right now. I am so upset and angry. I really want to hurt him/her, but I know that two wrongs don't make a right. God, you have to help me because I feel like I am going to explode. Show me how to handle this, dear God. Show me the right way to deal with this person and pain. Thank you, Lord, in Jesus's name.

Scripture for Meditation

"Do not repay evil for evil…"

(Romans 12:17).

"Wounds from a friend can be trusted, but an enemy multiplies kisses"

(Proverbs 27:6).

Word of Wisdom

What's worse than an enemy who hurts you is a friend who betrays you. However, you must determine whether this friend is really an enemy or whether this friend just made a mistake or grievous error. Friends make mistakes, and in any relationship sometimes we hurt those whom we love most. Hopefully this will not be a relationship that is necessarily thrown away but possibly reconciled over time.

Because you may be in the midst of many emotions right now due to the betrayal or offense, take time to deal with your emotions and to clear your head. Step back for a moment to properly evaluate the situation and assess what has happened. After you have had time to calm down, seek to meet with this "friend" to discuss what happened and why it happened. Does the friend appear remorseful for what he or she has done? Has he or she apologized? Express your hurt and disappointment, and if necessary take time away from the friendship so that you can have time to heal. In the midst of it all, pray for your friendship, and ask God for wisdom and guidance. If this friendship can be repaired, seek reconciliation in the near future.

60. Healing from an Alcoholic Mother

My gracious and loving God,

I am not even sure what to say or how to pray regarding my mother. I am feeling so much guilt realizing that my mother has a sickness, and she really doesn't know the pain and damage that she has caused with her drinking. My mother needs help, dear God. She needs deliverance, or she will continue on a destructive path. And the truth is, I can't keep putting myself in a position to be hurt, abused, or mistreated by my mother.

Lord, I know that it is the alcohol that affects my mother's behavior, but how long do I have to subject myself to my mother's behavior? How long do I have to experience the sting of her harsh and brutal words when she is intoxicated? I love my mother, dear God, but I don't like her. I don't like how she treats me. I am her daughter, but the things that she has said and done to me over the years no daughter should have to experience from their own mother. I know, God, that it is a sickness, but her behavior is poisonous when she drinks.

I ask you, dear Lord, to please heal my heart from this pain. Heal me from memories that have scarred me. Help me to not one day hate my mother. Heal us both, dear Lord. In Jesus's name.

Scripture for Meditation

"For he does not willingly bring affliction or grief to anyone"

(Lamentations 3:33).

"Praise be to the God and Father of our Lord Jesus Christ, the Father of compassion and the God of all comfort, who comforts us in our troubles…"

(2 Corinthians 1:3–4).

Word of Wisdom

I am glad that you recognize that alcoholism is a disease. Moreover, the effects of alcoholism can have detrimental consequences not only for the alcoholic but also for those who are affected by the person's alcoholism. Although you recognize it as a disease, it does not mean that you have to subject yourself to your mother's abuse when she is under the influence of alcohol. Inform your mother that you love her, but because of her hurtful words when she has been drinking, you refuse to be around her at those times. Loving your mother does not mean that you must suffer silently from her alcoholism.

Pray that your mother gets the help that she needs, and if necessary find a support group or a pastor to have an opportunity to express your pain and sorrow. Also ask God to heal your heart and to help you love your mother, even if it is from a distance until she gets the help that she needs. Lastly, believe in the power of intercession. In the midst of your healing, pray for your mother.

61. Healing from Pain That I Have Caused Others

Merciful God,

I need your mercies. I need your forgiveness, and I need your grace. I have done things in life that I am not proud of. I have hurt people. I have used people. I have betrayed people's trust. I admit to you, O God, that I have not always done right, but I plead to you for forgiveness and mercy. There are things that I have done that cannot be undone, but I do ask that if I have hurt (specific name) with my actions and words, please heal him/her of any pain that I may have caused.

I also ask you, dear God, to bless me with a fresh start and new beginning. Show me how to live, walk, talk, and love. Show me kindness, dear God. I want to change my life and become a better person. I want to prove to myself that I don't have to be a victim of my environment, and just because I may have been hurt in life, doesn't mean that I have a right to hurt others. Forgive me, O God, for anyone that I have disappointed, but I know that you can transform any life, including mine.

So I surrender to you, Lord. I admit that I cannot do this on my own, and I am willing to lean on you and trust your guidance. I thank you for forgiving me, and may I forgive myself as I seek to walk in a new direction. Bless your name forever. In Jesus's name.

Scripture for Meditation

"The Lord is compassionate and gracious, slow to anger, abounding in love. He will not always accuse, nor will he harbor his anger forever; he does not treat us as our sins deserve or repay us according to our iniquities"

(Psalm 103:8–10).

Word of Wisdom

God loves a repentant soul! You acknowledge that you have caused others pain by the choices that you have made in your life. It is wonderful that you desire a new walk and life in the Lord. Do know that although you are seeking a new life with Christ, it does not necessarily mean that others are going to suddenly begin to trust you. Trust will grow as others begin to see changes in your life and behavior.

However, that should not be your focus right now. Seek to nurture your relationship with Christ. Find a home church if you do not have one, and allow God to begin the process of transforming your life. If there are close relationships that have been damaged, ask God to give you the wisdom that you need to seek forgiveness or to apologize to those whom you've hurt or disappointed. Refuse to walk in self-judgment, guilt, or condemnation. The past is over and cannot be undone. Look forward to a new and wonderful life in Christ. God has a glorious future that awaits you.

62. Healing from Death of a Loved One

My God, this pain is unbearable. This is more than I can handle. When will the pain end? I feel like I will never recover from this hole in my soul. I feel like a part of me has died too. How am I supposed to go on? How can I go back to normal when my life has forever changed? How can I laugh again? It doesn't even seem right to go on living without ___(person's name)___.

Dear God help me to get through this. Please don't leave me in this pit of despair! I won't be able to go on unless you carry me. Please, Lord, be my strength. Comfort me, and wrap your arms around me. Stay close to me so that I don't feel even more alone. Help me get through this, dear Lord, because this hurts so bad. I need you, Lord.

Scripture for Meditation

"May your unfailing love be my comfort, according to your promise to your servant"

(Psalm 119:50).

Word of Wisdom

The death of a loved one is painful. It does hurt, and life does change when that person is no longer a part of your life. There is no easy way to get through the loss. You simply have to take it one day at a time as you grieve. Because the grieving process can take years, you may want to consider attending a grief-recovery support group to help you through the many emotions you may experience. A grief-recovery support group will give you ways to cope with the loss so that you do not become paralyzed by the grief. Also continue to pray to God for continued strength and comfort that he graciously provides to those who call on him.

63. Healing from Loss of a Job

Dear Lord,

In the midst of my pain, I bless your name. In the midst of my confusion, I give you praise, for I know that even during the difficulties of life, you are still God, and you are still good. Although I don't understand why I had to lose my job, I am trusting that you are in control of my life.

But, Lord, I need you to help me to get through this. Help me to hold on to everything that I worked so hard to get. Help me to be strong and to hold on to my faith. You know, O God, what I stand to lose by not having a job. So please, God, help me to keep a roof over my head. Please do not let me lose my car or fall behind on bills.

I ask you, dear God, to supply all of my needs. Bless me with a new job, my Lord, that can sustain me. I know that you are a provider, O God, and so I put this situation in your hands. I know that I can't get my old job back, and I trust that what you have for me will help me to forget the pain of what I lost. Please do not allow me to grow bitter that I had to lose my job but instead help me to look forward to what lies ahead.

Thank you, my God, for hearing my prayers as I am reminded that you are the one who provides for my every need. In Jesus's name. Amen.

Scripture for Meditation

"Do not be anxious about anything, but in everything, by prayer and petition, with thanksgiving, present your requests to God. And the peace of God, which transcends all understanding, will guard your hearts and minds in Christ Jesus"

(Philippians 4:6–7).

Word of Wisdom

No one likes having to lose a job because we are dependent upon our jobs to help provide for our needs, but unfortunately sometimes jobs close or layoffs occur. It is okay to grieve the loss of a job especially if it was a job that you enjoyed doing, a job that you've spent many years on, or a job that provided a great income for you and your household.

Because this door has now closed, you must determine what opportunities may await you. Is this an opportunity to change careers, to go back to school, or to venture out and start your own business? Be prayerful for direction and guidance. If your family or household is in dire need of income now, you may have to consider a lesser paying job or a different kind of job to hold you over until you find the right job. Seek to stay encouraged, trust God, and see this as an opportunity for a new door to open in your life.

64. Healing from Losing My House

My Dear God,

I am trying so hard not to grieve, but I never imagined losing my house. I thought that I would have this house forever. I just can't believe the place that I called home is no longer mine. I can't understand why you allowed me to get a house that I wouldn't be able to keep. I am trying to make sense of losing a house that I prayed for and worked so hard to get. Sometimes I just feel like a failure and feel embarrassed that I couldn't keep my house.

Lord, I feel like I am going backward instead of moving forward. I am really trying to hold on to my faith, but my home is gone. I know, Lord, that you are in control, but help me, Lord, to trust you because I know that you could've provided me with a miracle to keep my house. Please, dear Lord, keep me close and don't let me feel ashamed. Help me to heal. Please give me my joy back. I am believing that despite how things look, Lord, you will not fail me.

I bless your name forever and ever. In Jesus's name. Amen.

Scripture for Meditation

"You turned my wailing into dancing; you removed my sackcloth and clothed me with joy"

(Psalm 30:11).

Michele Teague-Humphrey

Word of Wisdom

Unfortunately in life we deal with losses. Sometimes those losses are due to our own actions, and at other times they are due to circumstances beyond our control. It is difficult to lose something that you have invested much time and money in, and of course, more than the monetary investment, memories were created in that home. The good thing is that your memories can go with you, and you can look forward to creating new memories in the next chapter of your life. It does not necessarily ease the pain of losing your home, but what it does mean is that you can pick up from where you left off and keep pressing forward to what awaits you in your future. Losing your home does not mean that you have to lose your hopes and dreams. It's okay to grieve, but also look forward to something better in the horizon.

65. Healing from Absent Mother

Gracious and loving God,

I come before you acknowledging you as God of all and God of my life. I honestly can't imagine where I would be now if you were not in my life. It is you, God, who has been my strength and support. You've kept me holding on when I have wanted to give up. But now, O God, I know it's time for my healing. I know that I have to be able to heal and forgive so that I can move on with my life.

But, dear God, I feel so stuck. I can't get away from the pain of my mother not being in my life the way that a mother should be. She abandoned me, God. She left me alone. I feel that she just walked out on me physically and emotionally. Did she even care about me? And if she didn't, then why even give birth to me? I need you, Lord, because I have a hole in my soul. I need you to heal me so that I don't feel this animosity toward my mother. I want to understand why she doesn't want a relationship with me, but, God, help me to just accept the fact that she chooses not to be in my life.

Hold me close, dear God. Wipe my tears away. Strengthen me with your love. Make me whole so that I can enjoy the life that you have blessed me with. Help me to embrace the friends and family that you have placed in my life. Thank you, my dear God, for hearing my prayer. In the wonderful name of Jesus I pray. Amen.

Scripture for Meditation

"Though my father and mother forsake me, the LORD will receive me"

(Psalm 27:10).

Word of Wisdom

In a perfect world we would have the perfect parents, but unfortunately we live in an imperfect world with imperfect people as well as imperfect parents. Because we live in an imperfect world, life does not always turn out the way that we desire to. Therefore things do not always happen in the way in which we think that they ought to happen. The truth is parenthood does not come with a manual. There is no test that one takes to determine if one is capable of being a father or mother. We make the assumption that if someone has a child, then he or she will automatically be excited and greatly look forward to parenthood. However, that is not always so. Some men and women are incapable of parenting or incapable of loving because of something within them.

You may have to live with unanswered questions. Life does not always provide the answers that we need nor does God always help us to make sense of our lives. All you can do is trust God and know that not having a mother to love you does not make you deficient in any way nor does it mean that there is something wrong with you. God allowed you to be born. Embrace the relationships that God has brought into your life, and recognize that your life is a gift to the world, with or without your mother.

66. Healing from Molestation

Holy and magnificent God,

Glory and honor to your name forever and ever. I worship you as creator and as my God who keeps me and watches over me day and night. I honor you as my Heavenly Father who loves me with unconditional love. I thank you, Lord, that you are near and close to me. You are never far away, and your ear is always attentive to my cries. Thank you, O God, for loving me too much to leave me alone.

I pray to you, my God, because I can't seem to heal from the pain of being molested. The memories still haunt me. I just don't understand how someone can do evil to a child. I don't understand how I could be sexually abused and have my innocence stolen from me. Lord, I feel like I have been robbed of my childhood. Things happened to me that should never happen to a child.

I try so hard to move on, but it is so tough, Lord. I wish it had never happened, but it did, and I keep reliving it. Please help me to press through the pain and to not allow the past to rob me of my future. Please help me not to allow the pain of yesterday to hinder my ability to experience peace and joy in my life. I am calling on you, Lord, because although I can't change my past, you can heal me. You can renew me and help me to not see myself as damaged. You can help my grieving spirit. I need you,

Lord, and I trust that you will empower me to get through this and to overcome it. Thank you for your pure love because you are my strength. In Jesus's name I pray. Amen.

Scriptures for Meditation

"My soul is weary with sorrow; strengthen me according to your word"

(Psalm 119:28).

Word of Wisdom

Some painful memories never go away, but we simply learn how to live with them. Yet God is able to subdue the pain so that the pain does not paralyze us or hinder us from moving forward with our lives. Although what happened to you in the past was evil and should not have happened, know that you do not have to be defined by your past. Consider speaking to a grief counselor or other licensed counselor who can help you through the grieving process of the molestation and also can help you to move forward.

As you continue to pray to God for divine healing, and as you progress in your healing, discover if God may want you to use your story to raise awareness of this act of evil that takes place in many homes and families where children are oftentimes left scarred and broken, and perpetrators go unpunished. Even if that is not God's will for your life, know that healing is!